D1191898

THE MEASUREMENT OF INTELLIGENCE OF INFANTS AND YOUNG CHILDREN

REVISED 1960

By

PSYCHE CATTELL, Ed.D.

THE PSYCHOLOGICAL CORPORATION
NEW YORK, N. Y.
1940

Reprinted with the permission of Psyche Cattell, Ed.D.

HNSON REPRINT CORPORATION
Fifth Avenue, New York, N. Y. 10003

JOHNSON REPRINT COMPANY LTD.
Berkeley Square House, London, W. 1

Second printing 1947
Third printing 1950
Fourth printing 1960

First reprinting 1966, Johnson Reprint Corporation
Printed in the United States of America

To

WALTER FENNO DEARBORN

Teacher and Friend

The material required for the administration of the infant tests described herein may be obtained from The Psychological Corporation, 304 East 45th Street, New York 17, N. Y.

FOREWORD

The psychometric examinations upon which this work has been based were part of a series of observations of children enrolled from birth for continuing and comprehensive study by the Department of Child Hygiene of the Harvard School of Public Health. This study, as well as the special research organization through which it was carried out, was made possible by a grant from the General Education Board. The periodic psychometric examination of these children was provided for in order to add to existing knowledge as to the variability in the pattern of mental growth as encountered among individuals and as revealed by these tests. It was also expected that they might give evidence as to the influence of environmental and health factors upon the progress of mental growth. It soon became evident that modification of the tests previously described as applicable to young children was necessary as a preliminary step toward accomplishing these objectives. It seemed desirable to construct a uniform testing program applicable to the years under study and comparable with the revised Stanford-Binet test adapted for older children.

It must be left to psychologists to determine with what measure of success Dr. Cattell has carried out this purpose in the present work. As a pediatrician I have been impressed with the need for simplification and orderly orientation of present procedures if psychometric testing is to serve its greatest practical usefulness. As Director of the Research Center at which Dr. Cattell carried out these studies, I have had an opportunity to appreciate the enormous amount of labor required and the painstaking precision with which Dr. Cattell has dealt with all aspects of this study. Many of the original objectives of her work were of necessity abandoned in order to complete this undertaking in a satisfactory manner, and a major portion of her time while on the staff at the Center during a seven-year period was devoted to this work.

Dr. Cattell has given credit to the members of the research staff of the Department of Child Hygiene at the Harvard School of Public Health for their part in making these studies possible. In these cooperative undertakings each worker is dependent upon many others for his results. The tasks of follow-up and of giving health service, which were essential requirements for regular retesting and for the maintenance of parental interest, fell to others on the staff. The parents themselves deserve recognition for their cooperative assistance. It is hoped that the effort expended in the preparation of these new test procedures will prove to have been justified by the greater satisfaction resulting from their use.

HAROLD C. STUART, M.D.,
Director, Harvard Center for Research in Child Health and Development

June 7, 1940

CONTENTS

Chapter I

INTRODUCTION

The data for the standardization of the Developmental and Intelligence Scale, which are being presented herewith, were obtained at the Center for Research in Child Health and Development conducted by the Department of Child Hygiene of the School of Public Health of Harvard University.[1] This Center was established in 1930 under the direction of Dr. Harold C. Stuart, and since that time an extensive study of the health and development of a group of normal children has been in progress. The original plan was to have the children brought to the Center every three months during the first year after birth and twice a year thereafter

[1] Every member of the Center has assisted in one way or another in making the completion of the Developmental and Intelligence Scale possible. Most directly concerned have been Miss Vernette S. Vickers, who administered 322 of the psychological examinations, and Dr. Mary M. Shirley, who administered 257. Dr. Harld C. Stuart, Dr. Mary Shirley, Miss V. S. Vickers, Miss M. J. Pottinger, Mrs. Bertha S. Burke, Mrs. Lydia Kennard, and Miss Alice Raymond have all read the manuscript, in part or in full, and have contributed toward its improvement. From outside the Center, the author is greatly indebted to Professor Walter F. Dearborn, Professor Lewis M. Terman, Professor Maud A. Merrill, and Professor Philip J. Rulon, who have read the manuscript and offered valuable suggestions. The photographs were taken by Mr. Armheim of the Psychological Corporation and Mr. Jaques Cattell.

as long as they remained enrolled at the Center. Later two additional routine visits were added, one at six weeks, and another at fifteen months. At each of these visits the child was given a series of examinations by specialists in the various fields. This has in most instances included a psychological, a medical, an orthopedic, a dental, and an anthropometric examination, a blood sample, a nutrition history, a series of photographs and x-ray films, and playroom observations. For a detailed account of the activities of the Center, the scope of the various examinations, and the groups of children under study, the reader is referred to a previous report.[2] The present study deals only with the results of the psychometric measurements of the Normal Child Series between the ages of three and thirty-six months.

The individuals to be enrolled in the Normal Child Series were selected during the prenatal period, by a public health nurse, from the pregnant women attending the clinics of the Boston Lying-in Hospital. The four main requirements for enrollment in the study were:

1. That all evidence should point toward the normal delivery of a normal child.

[2] Publication No. 1 of the Center for Research in Child Health and Development of the Harvard School of Public Health. Society for Research in Child Development, National Research Council, Washington, D. C.

2. That the father of the child should have employment which gave promise of permanence, and that he would be likely to reside near the Center for a number of years.

3. That at least three grandparents be of North European stock.

4. That the mother be able to give evidence of her ability and willingness to cooperate with the Center over a period of years.

Such a method of selection obviously could not result in an entirely random sample. Prospective mothers who had an income above a certain amount were not admitted to the clinics from which selection was made, so that "well-to-do" families were not enrolled. On the other hand, a sum of approximately $50.00 was required for entrance to the prenatal clinic, for delivery and care in the Boston Lying-in Hospital, so that those families in the lowest economic levels were excluded. Limiting the cases selected to those whose fathers held more or less permanent positions and whose mothers could give evidence of ability and willingness to cooperate with the Center over a period of years also had the effect of eliminating children whose parents were socially and mentally inadequate. The majority of the resulting group came from the lower middle classes and was made up to a considerable extent of the children of policemen, store-keepers, taxi-cab drivers, clerks, and the like. The mothers, before marriage, had in most cases worked as telephone operators, sales clerks, maids, and in similar occupations; a few had been teachers, nurses, or social workers.[3]

Up to October 11, 1937, 294 children had been enrolled in the Normal Child Series. At that time, 110 boys and 113 girls, or a total of 223, were still active members of the study: 37 of the 71 who left were dropped on account of unsatisfactory cooperation, the majority during the first year of their enrollment. The remaining 34 were dropped for unavoidable and unpredictable causes; 15 moved out of the city, and 12 others were either stillborn or died during infancy from congenital defects.

When the writer was called upon to select psychological tests for the measurement of mental development to be repeated at stated intervals, the construction of a new test was not considered. It was only after using the then existing tests for several years that it became evident that they could be improved with the aid of the data that had already been collected. The construction of a new scale was then planned.

[3] For a more detailed description of the construction of the group, see Publication No. 1 of the Center for Research in Child Health and Development of the Harvard School of Public Health. Society for Research in Child Health and Development, National Research Council, Washington, D. C.

During the first three years of this research, the Gesell tests were used between the ages of three and eighteen months and were administered and scored in accordance with prescribed procedures in so far as they could be determined from the directions given in "Mental Growth of the Preschool Child."[4] Just as the oldest children reached their second birthday, the Minnesota Preschool Scale[5] became available and was used at the ages of twenty-four and thirty months. At three years of age the Merrill-Palmer Scale of Mental Tests[6] was given. None of these tests was entirely satisfactory for the ages at which it was used, but nothing more satisfactory was at the time available. During the fourth year of the study the tests described below were substituted between the ages of three and thirty months and Form L of the Stanford-Binet was substituted at three years.[7] The new revision of the Stanford-Binet was at that time not yet on the market, but was made available to the Center through the kindness of the authors.[8]

[4] Arnold Gesell: *The Mental Growth of the Preschool Child.* New York: Macmillan Co. 1925.

[5] Florence Goodenough, Josephine C. Foster and M. J. von Wagenen. Minneapolis: Educational Test Bureau. 1932.

[6] Rachell Stutzmann: *Mental Measurement of Preschool Children.* Yonkers, N. Y.: World Book Co. 1931.

[7] A study of the tests used above the age of three years is reserved for a later report.

[8] Lewis M. Terman and Maud Merrill: *Measuring Intelligence.* Boston: Houghton Mifflin. 1937.

The Merrill-Palmer test is absorbingly interesting to most children of four and five years of age, but for the child of three it proved to be of little interest, especially to those who were a little below average in mental or manipulative ability. It was at times difficult or impossible to keep the child's attention on his task to the end of the time limit set by the author of the test. In addition to the limitation for children as young as three years the score on the Merrill-Palmer is more dependent on manipulative skill than is desirable for a test used as a measure of general intelligence. In the majority of cases the mental ages and I.Q.s obtained by use of the Merrill-Palmer scale agreed with those obtained by means of other tests, such as the Stanford-Binet or the Minnesota Preschool Scale. There were, however, a number of exceptions, where unusual skill or retardation in the development of the use of the hands was not accompanied by a similar acceleration or retardation in general intelligence. Case No. 35 (Percy T.) is an extreme example. (See Figure 1.) Most of his test results indicate a general mental development well above average, but markedly below the ratings obtained on the Merrill-Palmer Scale. Excluding the two Merrill-Palmer I.Q.s, the remaining eight I.Q.s between the ages of 12

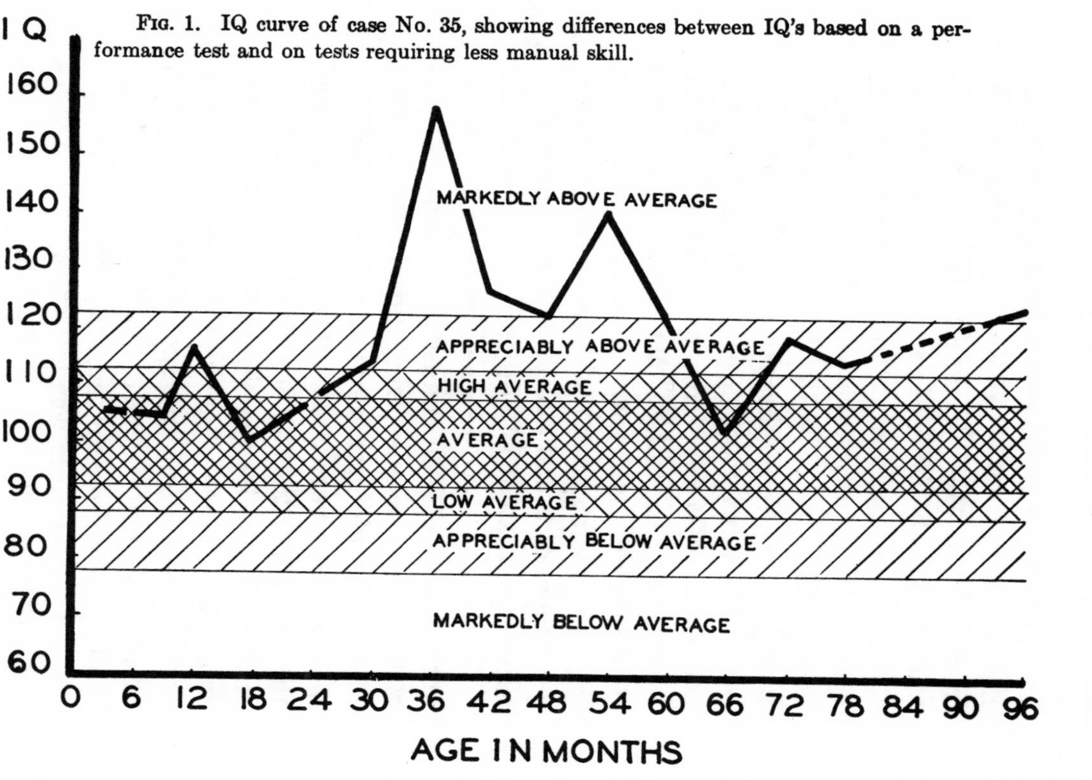

FIG. 1. IQ curve of case No. 35, showing differences between IQ's based on a performance test and on tests requiring less manual skill.

and 78 months average 116, the highest being 123, the lowest 100. At the age of three years he attained a Merrill-Palmer I.Q. of 158 and at four and one-half one of 140. If he had not "hit the top" of the test at four and one-half he would, no doubt, have earned an I.Q. more nearly comparable with the 158 he made at three years. With the exception of buttoning buttons, where he lost three points, his score was perfect. Approximately one hundred children were given a Merrill-Palmer test at three and at four and one-half years and even though the I.Q.s in general agreed with the other tests there were more dips and humps on the I.Q. curves at these ages than at any others.

The Minnesota Preschool Scale, while apparently having been unusually carefully constructed and standardized, did not prove satisfactory for children as young as two and two and one-half years. It did not catch and hold the interest of the shy or antagonistic child, and it was possible for the child of two years to obtain half his score on one of two items, thus giving him a rating on a special skill rather than on general mental development. There was also no provision for the adjustment of the total score when an item was lost through the child's lack of cooperation or from other causes. In order to obtain a final rating every item had to be scored plus or minus.[9]

The directions for giving and scoring the Gesell tests were not sufficiently detailed and objective to insure comparable results from different examiners and they lend themselves to descriptive rather than to numerical ratings. This is sometimes satisfactory or even desirable in clinical practice but more objective ratings are advantageous for the scientific study of individual growth. A careful search through the literature in 1930, however, revealed no mental or developmental test for infants that even approached Gesell's in the amount of time and careful work expended on its construction. Dr. Gesell has done a vast amount of pioneer work in the field of mental, motor and social development of infants and its measurement. In 1929 he listed 195 items[10] which he uses in the appraisal of infants between the ages of three and thirty months, and a few years later he described a number of additional items.[11] The larger pro-

[9] In fairness to the test it should be stated that the drawbacks mentioned are serious only at the youngest ages and that the test was found to be satisfactory for older children.

[10] Arnold Gesell: *Infancy and Human Growth.* New York: Macmillan. 1929.

[11] Arnold Gesell, Helen Thompson and Catherine Strunk Amatruda: *Infant Behavior: Its Genesis and Growth.* New York: Macmillan Co. 1938.

portion of these items was devised by Gesell himself or by his co-workers. This battery of tests has been used as a foundation for the scale described below.

The greatest weakness of the existing tests for children between the ages of eighteen and thirty months has been in their lack of appeal to the child. No matter how good a potential indicator of mental development a series of test items may be they cannot be satisfactory if the performance they require from the child is not of interest to him. No amount of praise and coaxing will persuade the majority of children between the ages of two and three years to put forth their best efforts if they do not enjoy the activity for its own sake, the tests then become a measure of interest rather than of ability. The items for the tests for infants under the ages of eighteen or twenty-four months are of necessity more satisfactory in their appeal. The only way to secure satisfactory cooperation from an infant during a mental test is to select items to which he will respond for his own pleasure. An infant of twelve months, for example, cannot be sat before a table and asked to perform one task after another against his wishes. Unless the task is such that he enjoys the performance for its own sake he will withdraw his cooperation and leave the examiner stranded. The most important factors contributing toward the unsatisfactoriness of the available infant tests were found to be the following:

1. The lack of objective procedures for administering and scoring the items, due in part to the types of items selected and in part to the lack of clear, precise directions.

2. To the inclusion of a large proportion of items of a personal-social nature, the responses to which are influenced to a marked degree by home training.

3. The inclusion of a number of items which are indicators of the development of large motor control which are probably only indirectly related to mental development.

4. The lack of scaling which makes impossible other than descriptive ratings.

5. The small age range which the series of items covers.

6. The unequal distribution of the items over the age range covered.

7. Poor standardization.

All these weaknesses are, of course, not found in any one test. There is, however, not a single published test for infants to date (October, 1937) for which definite and precise standard directions for administering and scoring, comparable to those which almost invariably accompany a good test for children of school age, are given.

The only age scale similar to the Binet method

is that of Hetzer, Wolf and Kohler, developed in the laboratory of Charlotte Bühler at the University of Vienna.[12] Their tests were not considered satisfactory for the present study for several reasons. A large proportion of the standardization data was obtained from institution children and less than half of the items included are claimed to test mainly mental development. In addition, the scale includes items the purpose of which is to arouse displeasure or fear in the child. This is a questionable procedure at any time and especially when the cooperation of the child is desired for additional examinations.

Several investigators, including Fillmore,[13] Bailey,[14] and others, have scaled the Gesell tests or modifications of them by means of Thurstone's method of absolute scaling. They have all found an unequal distribution of items. Fillmore, for example, who eliminated all items of a personal-social type and included only a small number of tests of large muscle control, such as sitting and standing, found one item between

[12] Charlotte Bühler: *The First Year of Life.* New York: The John Day Company. 1930.

[13] Eva A. Fillmore: *Iowa Tests for Young Children.* University of Iowa Studies. Studies in Child Welfare, Vol. XI, No. 4. Iowa City: The University of Iowa.

[14] Nancy Bailey: *Mental Growth During the First Three Years: A Developmental Study of Sixty-one Children by Repeated Tests.* Genetic Psychology Monographs, Vol. 14, No. 1. Worcester, Mass.: Clark University Press. 1933.

six and seven months and five between eleven and twelve months; none in the two months' interval between seventeen and one-half and nineteen and one-half months, but nine in the two months' interval between twenty and twenty-two months, and so on.

It was with a view to the construction of a test as free as possible from the seven limitations mentioned above, but still maintaining the good points of already existing tests, that the present work was undertaken. As stated above, the Gesell tests were used as a point from which to build. The items of the Gesell tests were first arranged in an age scale similar to that of the Stanford-Binet tests. In order to make the scale as much an intelligence scale as possible, over 100 items, the responses to which were thought to be unduly influenced by home training or to depend mainly on large muscular control, were eliminated. Other items collected from various sources were added to fill the gaps. All the directions for giving and scoring items have been rewritten in a detailed and in as objective a manner as possible. A large majority of the items taken from the Gesell tests were modified, more or less, in order to make the giving or scoring more objective, or to increase or decrease the difficulty for the purpose of attaining an equal number of items at each of the age levels covered. A total of 1346 examinations were used in connection with the standardization, but, unfortunately, those items which were added later were not given to as many children as were those used from the beginning.

The scale runs from two months to thirty months, but has been so constructed as to constitute an extension downward of Form L of the Stanford-Binet tests. Between the ages of twenty-two and thirty months Stanford-Binet items are intermingled with other items. Thus, using the infant test items for the early months and the Stanford-Binet Tests for the older ages with a mixture of the two between, one continuous scale from early infancy to maturity has been attained.

No claim is made that the present scale is perfect. Unfortunately, the funds available for this part of the study became exhausted before all the data that would have been desirable had been collected and a complete statistical analysis made. It is thought, however, that it is a step in the right direction and it is hoped that it will prove to be of value in clinical and scientific work until a revision and a re-standardization can be made.

CHAPTER II

STATISTICAL EVALUATION

The standardization of the tests is based on 1346 examinations made on 274 children at the ages of three, six, nine, twelve, eighteen, twenty-four, thirty and thirty-six months. As stated above, during the first three years of the study the Gesell tests, as described in "The Mental Growth of the Preschool Child,"[1] were given to children under two years. Later, the less satisfactory items from this test were discarded and a number of additional items added from other sources.

Unfortunately those items which were added later could not be given to as many children as those items used from the beginning. At times other factors also prevented giving every item appropriate to the child's mental level. In the interests of the study as a whole it was necessary to limit the time allotted to this examination to forty-five minutes. Lack of time sometimes made it necessary to omit some of the items in the age groups where a large number were being tried out. Whenever it was necessary to do so, care was taken that the selection be made in an objective manner. For example, for a period of time a

[1] Arnold Gesell. New York: Macmillan Co. 1925.

given set of items would be omitted when the time was short and during another period a different set. Another cause for an item not being given to all the children for which it was appropriate was the misplacement of an item in the trial arrangement. The "glass frustration" test is the most striking example. It was taken from Bühler's 1930 tests[2] and was placed at ten months as it had been placed in the Vienna Baby Tests. For the group of infants under consideration and the method of administration used the item was found to belong at the fourteen-month level. As a result of this misplacement it was only presented to a selected group of the appropriate age level. It was most frequently presented to children of nine months and to average or dull children of twelve months, almost all of whom failed to pass. Only occasionally was it given to the child whose mental age was near fourteen months. A number of other items were sufficiently misplaced in the trial arrangements to cause them to be administered to only a selected group of children of the appropriate age level. All data collected from similarly misplaced items were discarded. A few items that appeared to be promising had to be eliminated on account of the small number of cases of the appropriate age level to which they were administered.

[2] Charlotte Bühler: *The First Year of Life.* New York: The John Day Company. 1930.

The items were rearranged twice during the period in which the data was being collected. Over one hundred items which were found to be unsatisfactory for one or more of the following reasons were eliminated:

1. Items which showed insufficient increase in the percentage of passes from one age group to the next.
2. Items which increased irregularly in the number of passes from age to age, which showed plateaus or failed to approach closely the 100% mark at any age.
3. Items which were difficult to administer or to score, or which required an undue amount of subjective judgment on the part of the examiner.
4. Items which did not hold the attention of the child.
5. Items requiring cumbersome apparatus.
6. Items which were thought to be appreciably influenced by home training.
7. Items planned primarily to test control of the large muscle groups and which do not correlate well with the scale as a whole.
8. Items which appeared to test abilities similar to those covered by another item at the same age level.
9. Items at age levels for which a sufficient number of more or equally satisfactory items were available.

The final arrangement contains five regular test items and either one or two alternates at each of the age levels two, three, four, five, six, seven, eight, nine, ten, eleven, twelve, fourteen, sixteen, eighteen, twenty, twenty-two, twenty-four, twenty-seven and thirty months. The alternate items are second choices which are not quite as satisfactory as those numbered from one to five but which may be substituted for them when one has been spoiled in the process of giving through the child's lack of cooperation or through other causes.

Although the test has been standardized on and constructed for use with children at the ages of three, six, nine, twelve, eighteen, twenty-four and thirty months, the indications are that it may be used with only a little less accuracy with children between these ages. However, data on which these indications are based are so meager that until more data become available the tests at these "between ages" should be interpreted with extra caution (see page 40). The placements of items between these ages were estimated. For example, the items placed at fourteen and sixteen months are those that were proved to be too difficult for the age of twelve months and too easy for the age of eighteen months. As nearly as could be estimated they are appropriate for ages fourteen and sixteen months, respectively. Those items placed at fourteen months were passed by a larger proportion of the twelve- and eighteen-month-old children than were those placed at sixteen. The percentage of twelve-month-old children passing each of the fourteen- and sixteen-month items varied from eleven to forty-three and from zero to thirty, respectively, and for the eighteen-month-old children from ninety-one to ninety-eight and eighty-three to ninety, respectively. The placement of other items between the age groups tested were estimated in a similar manner. The percentage of children passing each item at each of the age levels to which they were administered is given in Table 1.

In order to obtain some indication of the accuracy of the placement of the "between-age-group" items, about twenty-five of the mothers of the children enrolled at the Center were asked if they would be interested in bringing their children in for an examination every month during the first year. The extra visits were entirely voluntary, but it was made clear to the mothers that we only wished them to start the extra visits if they thought they would be sufficiently interested to continue them throughout the year. At the end of the first year they were invited to bring the children in every two months during the second year,

TABLE 1

PERCENTAGE OF CHILDREN PASSING EACH ITEM AT EACH AGE LEVEL

	3 Months		*6 Months*		*9 Months*		*12 Months*	
	Total No.	Per cent passing	Total No.	Per cent passing	Total No.	Per cent passing	Total No.	Per cent passing
Two Months								
1. Voice, attends	98	100						
2. Inspects environment	198	98						
3. Ring, follows continuous horizontal	204	99						
4. Follows moving person	206	98						
5. Babbles	202	95						
Alt. a. Ring, follows vertical	61	97						
Alt. b. Head, lifts in prone								
Three Months								
1. Ring, follows in circle	58	90						
2. Feeding, anticipates (bottle)	100	80	67	100				
3. Cube, regards	197	79	67	100				
4. Fingers, inspects	187	76	67	100				
5. Spoon, regards	195	82	67	100				
Alt. a. Chest, lifts by arms	186	63	67	100				
Alt. b. Head erect and steady	190	87						

TABLE 1—(*Continued*)

	3 Months		*6 Months*		*9 Months*		*12 Months*	
	Total No.	Per cent passing	Total No.	Per cent passing	Total No.	Per cent passing	Total No.	Per cent passing
Four Months								
1. Hands, manipulates	206	57	67	100				
2. Hands, open	183	61	67	100				
3. Ball, follows	78	36	67	99				
4. Voice, turns to	78	4	64	99				
5. Increased activity, at sight of toy	85	31	64	100				
Alt. a. Rattle, recovers from chest	82	5	64	98				
Alt. b. Rattle active play	159	0.4	172	96				
Five Months								
1. Bell, turns to	77	0	172	89	168	99		
2. Ring, attains	123	4	167	89	168	99		
3. Transfers object from hand to hand	19	0	68	87	168	99		
4. Pellet, regards	20	0	176	84	168	99		
5. Spoon, picks up	195	0	66	85	168	100		
Alt. a. Ring, pulls down	121	2	66	80	168	100		
Alt. b. Paper, crumples			85	84	168	99		

TABLE 1—(*Continued*)

	3 Months		*6 Months*		*9 Months*		*12 Months*	
	Total No.	Per cent passing	Total No.	Per cent passing	Total No.	Per cent passing	Total No.	Per cent passing
Six Months								
1. Cube, attains	197	0	181	79	168	100		
2. Cup, lifts	19	0	177	79	170	99		
3. Mirror, manipulates and approaches	20	0	167	80	170	99		
4. Reaching, unilateral	197	0	174	63	158	98		
5. Cube, approaches 2nd	197	0	26	77	113	100		
Alt. a. Reaching, persistent	197	0	177	62	170	95		
Seven Months								
1. Pellet, attempts			149	58	166	98		
2. Mirror, pats and smiles			163	50	152	97		
3. Ring, inspects			84	49	168	96		
4. Cube, takes two			66	45	83	93		
5. Paper, exploits			63	40	81	99		
Alt. a. String, grasps			43	28	57	100		
Alt. b. Peg, pulls out			34	38	46	85		

TABLE 1—(*Continued*)

	6 Months		*9 Months*		*12 Months*		*18 Months*	
	Total No.	Per cent passing	Total No.	Per cent passing	Total No.	Per cent passing	Total No.	Per cent passing
Eight Months								
1. Ring, pulls by string	163	6	169	84	184	96		
2. String, interest	79	20	79	80	90	99		
3. Says "dada," etc.	181	9	164	82	191	99.5		
4. Pellet, rakes	175	10	167	92				
5. Bell, interest in details	63	1	156	82	90	97		
Alt. a. Hand preference	177	46	161	80				
Alt. b. Spoon, bangs	67	16	84	96				
Nine Months								
1. Pellet, scissor grasp	175	0	165	75	190	98		
2. Spoon, looks	170	9	159	75	92	98		
3. Bell, rings	76	4	164	58	174	86		
4. Adjusts to gesture	76	3	160	76	187	97		
5. Adjusts to words	76	0	150	63	189	96		
Alt. a. Imitates sounds	76	3	161	65	188	93		

TABLE 1—(*Continued*)

	6 Months		9 Months		12 Months		18 Months	
	Total No.	Per cent passing	Total No.	Per cent passing	Total No.	Per cent passing	Total No.	Per cent passing
Ten Months								
1. Toy, uncovers	18	0	82	58	87	97		
2. Cup and cube, combines	18	0	167	40	189	86		
3. Third cube, attempt	76	10	80	52	51	92		
4. Spoon-rattle, hits outside	18	0	81	35	89	94		
5. Peg board, fingers holes	62	6	80	59	89	98		
Alt. a. Spoon-cup, contacts spoon first			18	61	14	78		
Eleven Months								
1. Pellet, plucks			164	27	188	89		
2. Cup and cube, secures			170	22	191	81	117	100
3. Box and stones	18	0	56	15	69	81		
4. Words, one			163	12	191	78	160	99
5. Cube in or over cup			82	15	177	76	117	100
Alt. a. Doll, squeaks	18	6	52	50	51	92		

TABLE 1—(*Continued*)

	6 Months		*9 Months*		*12 Months*		*18 Months*	
	Total No.	Per cent passing	Total No.	Per cent passing	Total No.	Per cent passing	Total No.	Per cent passing
Twelve Months								
1. Spoon, imit. beating			84	16	89	66	117	99
2. Cubes, in cup, one, No.			61	5	50	70	59	98
3. Pencil, marks			82	2	192	67	118	97
4. Spoon, cup—rattle	18	0	163	5	190	58	69	98
5. Words, two			163	4	195	60	128	96
Alt. a. Doll, hits	18	6	152	32	183	69	115	94
Fourteen Months								
1. Words, three			81	0	188	40	170	92
2. Cube, unwraps			164	3	183	40	131	94
3. Glass			82	1	70	24	51	94
4. Pellet-bottle, imitates			82	0	90	11	98	91
5. Peg, out and in			80	0	83	24	72	97
Alt. a. Cube, takes third			161	5	190	40	148	98
Alt. b. Box, opens			73	1	79	43		

TABLE 1—(*Continued*)

	9 Months		12 Months		18 Months		24 Months	
	Total No.	Per cent passing	Total No.	Per cent passing	Total No.	Per cent passing	Total No.	Per cent passing
Sixteen Months								
1. Formboard, round block	162	2	186	30	183	94	74	99
2. Words, five	82	0	184	17	144	83	75	97.3
3. Marbles in box	82	0	80	25	94	93	74	100
4. Pellet-bottle, solves	82	0	183	13	185	83	73	99
5. Round box, shuts	82	0	80	11	92	86	74	100
Alt. a. Pegboard, urges	82	0	84	0	43	84	63	100
Alt. b. Imitation scribble	82	0	191	24	186	90	74	100
Eighteen Months								
1. Fills cup with 10 cubes			186	16	186	76	73	99
2. Doll, points to one			182	7	180	63	56	98
3. Formboard, rd. hole rev., 1			184	11	192	77	75	99
4. Pencil, scribble			178	6	185	70	74	99
5. Picture, points to one			68	6	182	64	59	93
Alt. a. Asks with words			87	1	187	65	76	95
Alt. b. Pegboard A					104	74	76	97

TABLE 1—(*Continued*)

	12 Months		*18 Months*		*24 Months*		*30 Months*	
	Total No.	Per cent passing	Total No.	Per cent passing	Total No.	Per cent passing	Total No.	Per cent passing
Twenty Months								
1. Tower of three	181	3	183	56	75	97	59	100
2. Formboard, square	186	5	183	54	74	95	87	100
3. Stick. attains object	30	0	58	53	39	95	68	100
4. Doll, points to three	28	0	135	29	28	97	30	100
5. Doll-chair, two	28	0	72	68	67	87	61	98
Alt. a. Delayed response			78	54	64	86	57	100
Alt. b. Pegboard B			106	42	75	93	60	100
Twenty-two Months								
1. Square box, shuts	95	0	96	28	68	90	48	100
2. Words, combines			182	34	116	91	58	100
3. Formboard, solves			180	18	81	82	87	100
4. Pictures, points to two			100	31	54	89	53	100
5. Doll-chair, 3			72	47	67	78	78	99
Alt. a. Identifies object by name, 2			84	29	66	86	59	95
Alt. b. Picture vocabulary, 1			149	26	70	79	58	98

TABLE 1—(*Continued*)

	18 Months		*24 Months*		*30 Months*		*36 Months*	
	Total No.	Per cent passing	Total No.	Per cent passing	Total No.	Per cent passing	Total No.	Per cent passing
Twenty-four Months								
1. Identifies objects by name, 4	74	11	66	65	59	97		
2. Paper, folds indefinitely	149	6	72	64	59	95		
3. Watch, incomplete, 3rd	108	6	46	67	53	83		
4. Simple commands (S–B), 2	66	15	71	73	61	90		
5. Names objects, 3	45	7	53	66	64	98		
Alt. a. Picture vocabulary, 3	149	3	70	69	58	93		
Alt. b. Cubes, replace in box	104	17	68	74	54	94		
Twenty-seven Months								
1. Train, blocks in row	164	2	74	34	58	86	8	
2. Egg beater	80	16	51	21	32	91		
3. Pencil, imitates stroke	174	11	70	50	59	88	15	
4. Picture vocabulary, 7	149	0	70	37	58	87	82	
5. Pictures, points to 6	126	0	53	53	53	91	17	
Alt. a. Names objects, 4	45	2	50	50	63	97	74	
Alt. b. Digits, 4–7, 6–3, 5–8, 1	68	3	79	29	92	84	80	

TABLE 1—(*Continued*)

	18 Months		24 Months		30 Months		36 Months	
	Total No.	Per cent passing	Total No.	Per cent passing	Total No.	Per cent passing	Total No.	Per cent passing
Thirty Months								
1. Tower-bridge	171	.6	81	6	58	67	32	
2. Pencil, H–V and S–C, 2	79	0	87	18	78	43	3	
3. Formboard, rotated, 1	53	2	85	27	55	65	81	
4. Paper, folds definitely	135	2	71	17	68	69	6	
5. Identifies by use, 4	88	0	55	16	69	49	79	
Alt. a. Pictures, points to 7	126	0	58	31	53	76	18	
Alt. b. Cube, just one	53	2	62	26	65	51	13	

and at the end of this year they were invited to continue for one more year, bringing the child in every three months. Over half the mothers asked accepted the invitation. All those still in the study at the end of the first and second years elected to continue for the additional year. The mothers faithfully fulfilled their side of the bargain. Very few failed to appear at the appointed time without good cause and only those who either moved to a greater distance from the Center or who again became pregnant dropped from the study. However, this left only ten cases with reasonably complete records at the end of three years. The selection of cases on the basis of the mother's evident willingness, interest, and ability to bring her child to the Center at short intervals resulted in a group of children with superior mental ability. The average I.Q. of the group, on Form L of the Stanford-Binet, was 118 at the age of thirty-six months with only three I.Q.s below 114. The median I.Q.s for each of twenty-one ages are shown in Figure 2.

The data available show a close agreement between the I.Q.s obtained at the ages at which the test was standardized and the "between-ages" after twelve months. The medians of the thirteen age groups above eleven months vary only from 111 to 119, suggesting that the "between-age"

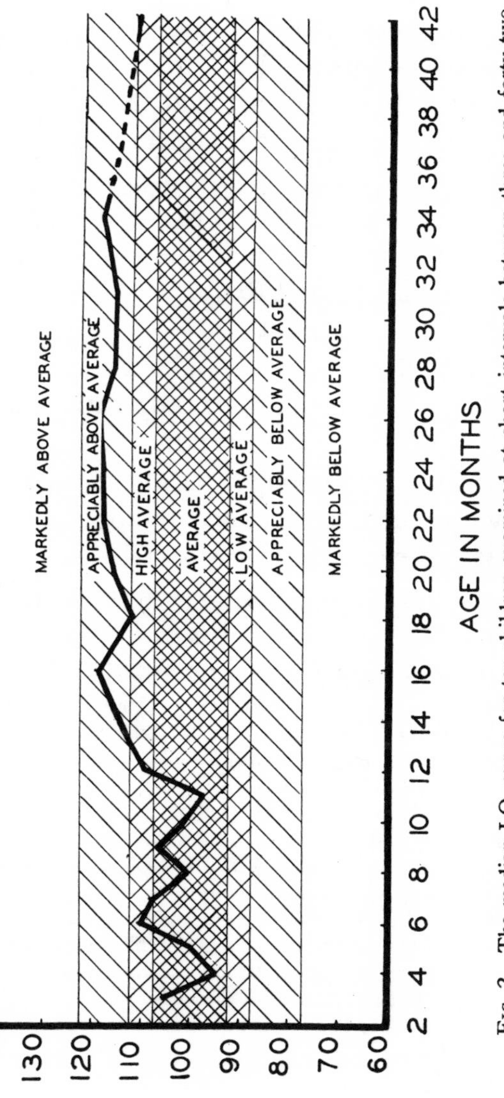

FIG. 2. The median I.Q. curve for ten children examined at short intervals between three and forty-two months of age.

items are satisfactorily placed. Below twelve months the results are less satisfactory, as would be expected from the fact that the tests are also less satisfactory at the ages of three, six and nine months than at any of the other ages at which the tests were standardized. Two of the dips in the curves, one at eight and the other at eleven months, may probably be explained by the fact that at each of these ages three of the ten children either missed the examination or the test was discarded on account of lack of cooperation from the infant. All three of the children who missed the eight-month tests stood among the highest four at the age of three years, and of those who missed the test at eleven months two stood among the first four and one stood sixth. Ages eight and eleven are the only ages at which there were as few as seven usable I.Q.s.[3] At four months all but two

[3] In three age groups two I.Q.s were missing. At the ages of sixteen and twenty months one of the children who missed the test was shown by later tests to be definitely below the median and the other above, so that it is probable that the median was not effected by their absence. At thirty-three months two of the brightest children missed the test; since their scores had been definitely above the median in the previous three and the following two tests (the last given) they were assumed to be above the median at thirty-three months. In one other instance a child who missed the test was used in obtaining the median. This child missed his twenty-month examination, but since he had made the lowest score in each of the other twelve age groups between eleven and forty-two months it was assumed that his score was below the median at twenty months.

of the ten I.Q.s were below 100, probably indicating that the tests are too advanced for this level.

There were thirty-five cases available who had been given the Infant Test at each of the seven age levels from three to thirty months and Form L of the Stanford-Binet at thirty-six months (approximately 250 examinations in all). As pointed out in Chapter I, the method of selection of cases to be enrolled at the Center was such that the average social level of the group as a whole was probably somewhat above that of the general population. The average Stanford-Binet I.Q., Form L, of the thirty-five cases at three years was 105. The test items were therefore placed in such a manner as to bring the median I.Q.s at the younger age groups as close as possible to that obtained with the Stanford-Binet at three years. The scoring and placement of items were modified and the tests rescored four times before the present arrangement was obtained. When the test items and scoring had been so arranged that the thirty-five cases who had nearly complete records had median I.Q.s as near as possible to their three-year, Stanford-Binet I.Q.s the test blanks for all other children who had been given the test between the ages of three and thirty months were scored on the same basis. The medians for this larger group are given in Table 2. At no age does the median I.Q. differ from that obtained on the Stanford-Binet by more than two points.

TABLE 2

MEDIAN I.Q.S

Infant Test I.Q.s from Three to Thirty Months Inclusive and Stanford-Binet I.Q.s at Thirty-six Months

Age	*F*	*I.Q.*
Months		
3	96	105
6	103	108
9	85	104
12	100	106
18	100	108
24	80	106
30	56	108
36*	63	106 (Stanford-Binet)

* The asterisk indicates that the I.Q.s are based on Form L of the Stanford-Binet. All others were obtained from the Infant Tests.

The median variations in I.Q. between one age group and the next are given in Table 3.

The median changes in I.Q. (signs disregarded) were found to be much larger before than after twelve months of age. Between the three-month intervals 3–6, 6–9, and 9–12 they range from 9.3 to 11.2. For the six-month intervals between twelve and thirty-six months the median differences are appreciably smaller, varying from 5.0 to 7.0. When signs were taken into account, the variations from one age interval to the next, be-

TABLE 3

I.Q. CHANGES BETWEEN SUCCESSIVE AGE GROUPS

Infant Test I.Q.s from Three to Thirty Months Inclusive and Stanford-Binet I.Q.s at Thirty-six and Forty-two Months

Age	*F*	*Signs disregarded*	*Signs considered*
Months			
3 – 6	60	10.5	+ 2.4
6 – 9	61	11.2	– 1.6
9 –12	58	9.3	– 0.2
12 –18	67	6.8	+ 2.1
18 –24	66	7.0	– 3.0
24 –30	51	6.5	+ 2.8
30 –36*	42	5.0	– 1.5
36*–42*	20	10.5	– 4.5

* See note to Table 2.

tween three and thirty-six months, varied from + 2.4 to – 3.0.

The tests for three months, as indicated by the correlation coefficients and the individual I.Q. curves, are neither very valid nor very reliable. The reliability coefficient obtained by the split-half method and corrected by the Spearman-Brown Formula is only 0.56, and the correlation between the score at three months and Form L of the Stanford-Binet at thirty-six months is only 0.10. The low reliability and validity coefficients of the tests for very young infants make it obvious that the individual numerical ratings must not be taken at their face value. The tests have not been omitted because, in spite of their low predictive value for the individual when used alone, as indicated by the coefficients, they may be of considerable assistance to the clinician in appraising an infant, especially in cases of extreme variation from the norm, and because insofar as the writer has been able to determine there are no others available that give more satisfactory results. It is also hoped that they may prove of value as a starting point for the construction of a more satisfactory test for very young infants.

In spite of the low reliability coefficients and the low validity coefficients for the three-month tests, an infant who earns a high developmental quotient at three months has appreciably better than average chances of being rated high at two or three years. The I.Q.s of the ten infants with reasonably complete records who received the highest rating at three months are plotted in open circles in Figure 3. Numbers have been placed inside the circles in order that the course of development of the individual child may be traced. Only one child fell below one hundred during the three-year period. Of the 62 tests given between three and thirty-six months, 45 resulted in I.Q.s of 110 or better, and only four I.Q.s, all belonging to one child, fell below 100.

On the other hand, the predictive value of an

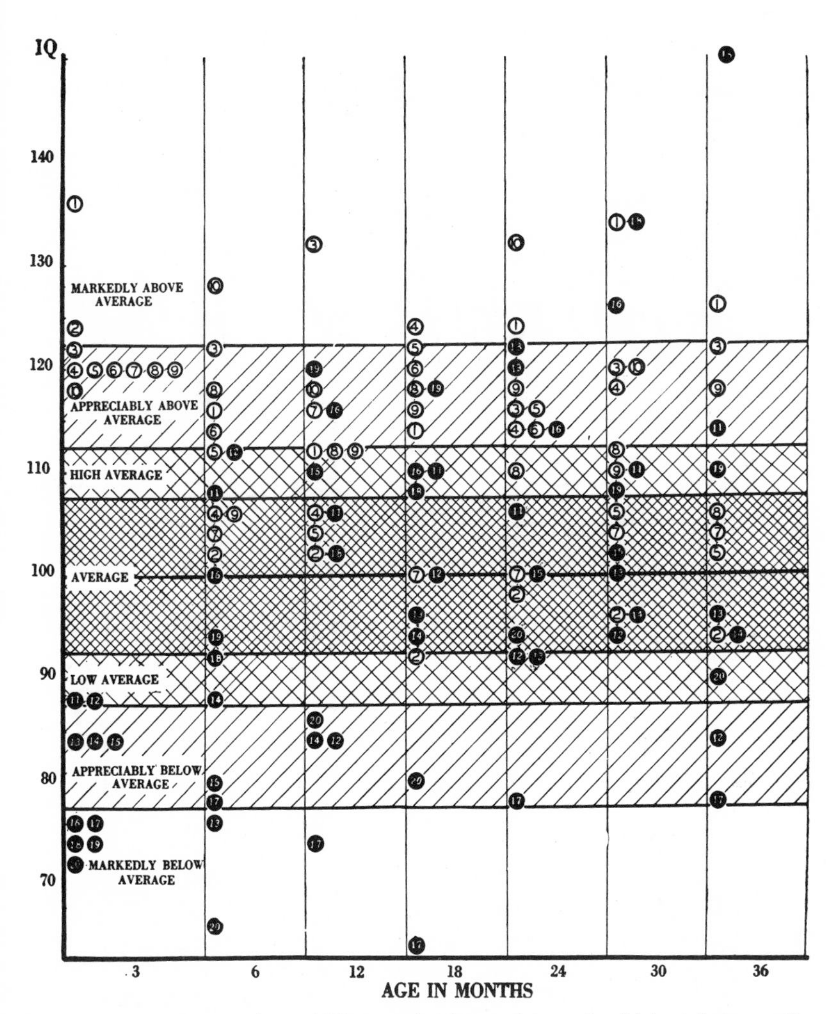

FIG. 3. Repeated tests of ten children testing low and ten tesing high at three months.

individual low rating at three months appears to be much too low for practical purposes. The ten cases with I.Q.s below 88 who had the most complete records showed wide variation in I.Q. as they became older, wider than would ordinarily be expected from a random group of ten cases. At thirty-six months the range was from 76 to 150; at thirty months six of the eight cases examined obtained an I.Q. of 100 or better. It may be tentatively concluded that a three-month-old infant who obtains a rating of 120 has much less than an average chance of rating below average at three years. On the other hand, a low rating at three months appears to give but little indication as to whether an individual child's future development will be above or below average, though his chances of rating below average are greater than those of an infant who rates average or better.

The tests at six, nine and twelve months show a marked increase in reliability, the reliability coefficients being 0.88, 0.86 and 0.89, respectively. The correlations with the Stanford-Binet at thirty-six months are 0.34, 0.18 and 0.56, respectively. At the ages eighteen, twenty-four and thirty months the reliability coefficients rise to 0.90, 0.85 and 0.71, and the correlation with the Stanford-Binet at thirty-six months is 0.67, 0.71 and 0.83, respectively. The reliability coefficient of sixty-two Stanford-Binet mental ages at three years calculated by the same method gave a coefficient of 0.87. The reliability coefficients of the

TABLE 4

RELIABILITY COEFFICIENTS
Calculated by the Odd-Even Procedure and Corrected for Length by Means of the Spearman-Brown Formula

No.	*Age*	*Coef.*
87	3 mos.	0.56 ± .05
100	6 "	0.88 ± .02
85	9 "	0.86 ± .02
101	12 "	0.89 ± .01
100	18 "	0.90 ± .01
80	24 "	0.85 ± .02
56	30 "	0.71 ± .05
62	36 " S.-B.	0.87 ± .02

TABLE 5

VALIDITY COEFFICIENTS
Correlation Coefficient between the Thirty-six Month Stanford-Binet, Form L, and Infant Examination

No.	*Age*	*Coef.*
42	3 mos. and 36 L	0.10 ± .10
49	6 " " 36 "	0.34 ± .08
44	9 " " 36 "	0.18 ± .10
57	12 " " 36 "	0.56 ± .06
52	18 " " 36 "	0.67 ± .05
52	24 " " 36 "	0.71 ± .05
42	30 " " 36* "	0.83 ± .03
19	42* " L " 36* "	0.75 ± .07
53	18 and 30 mo. infants	0.67 ± .05

*See note to Table 2.

Infant Tests thus compare favorably with the Stanford-Binet except at three and thirty months. No explanation has been found for the lower reliability coefficient at thirty months unless it be chance due to the smaller number of cases. The same data give a higher correlation with the Stanford-Binet at thirty-six months than do any of the other age groups, and the individual I.Q. curves give no indication of greater unreliability at this point.

It should be noted that the reliability coefficients were obtained by the split-half method and that in the construction of the test an effort was made to include as widely diversified items as possible at each age level, the purpose being to increase the validity of the test by sampling as many types of ability as possible. The deliberate selection of heterogeneous material for the test made it impossible to divide the test into anything like exactly comparable halves for the purpose of computing reliability coefficients. Therefore, the reliability coefficients presented are lower than would have been obtained if two comparable forms of the test had been available.

Only nineteen cases had been given a Stanford-Binet test at two different ages, namely at thirty-six and forty-two months. The correlation between the mental ages at these two levels was 0.75.

Those between the Stanford-Binet at thirty-six months and the Infant Test, at eighteen, twenty-four and thirty months average 0.73.[4] When it is considered that the average time interval was longer for the Infant Tests it may be concluded that the predictive value of the Infant Tests from eighteen months on also compare favorably with Form L of the new Stanford-Binet. It must, however, be emphasized that only nineteen repeated Stanford-Binet mental ages were available and that it is possible or, perhaps, even probable that an adequate sample would have given a higher validity coefficient.

The fact that the Infant Tests have markedly greater predictive value from eighteen months on than they do before twelve months is shown even more strikingly by the individual I.Q. curves shown in Figures 4 to 8. Each figure shows a random selection of five cases. It will be seen that the curves cross and recross in an apparently haphazard manner below twelve months, but after

[4] As pointed out above, it was not always possible to give all the items appropriate to his age to every child, on account of lack of time, fatigue of the child or the misplacement of items in the trial arrangement. As a result about 7% of the items used in the final scoring were alternates and even after an alternate had been substituted for each item missing, wherever one was available, the number of items on which the test was scored was still about 2.5% below what it should have been. It is probable that the reliability and validity coefficients would have been slightly higher if they could have been based on absolutely complete tests.

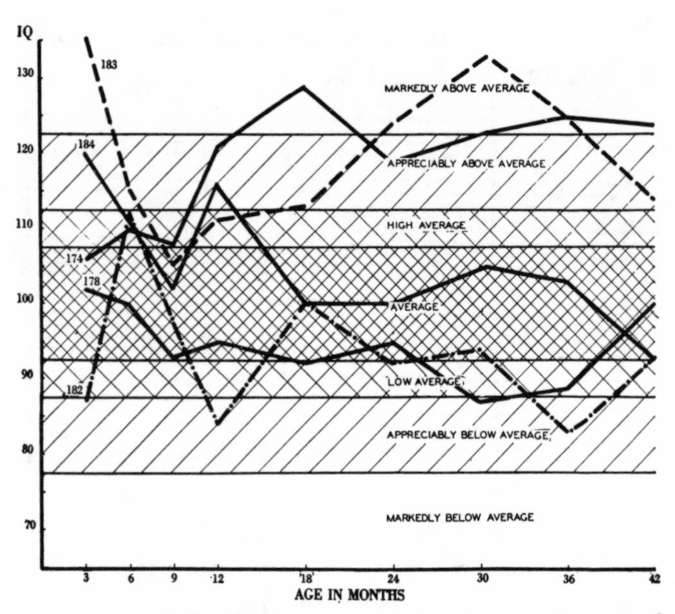

Fig. 4. Individual I.Q. curves of infants between the ages of three and forty-two months.

twelve months of age there is comparatively little crossing of the curves. For most of the cases plotted in Figures 4, 5 and 6 a Stanford-Binet, Form L, I.Q. was obtained at both thirty-six and forty-two months. It will be noted that the individual I.Q. curves show an approximately equal amount of variation between the I.Q.'s obtained with the Infant Test at six-month intervals from eighteen to thirty months and the Infant Test I.Q. at thirty months and that of the Stanford-Binet at thirty-six months as between the Stanford-Binet

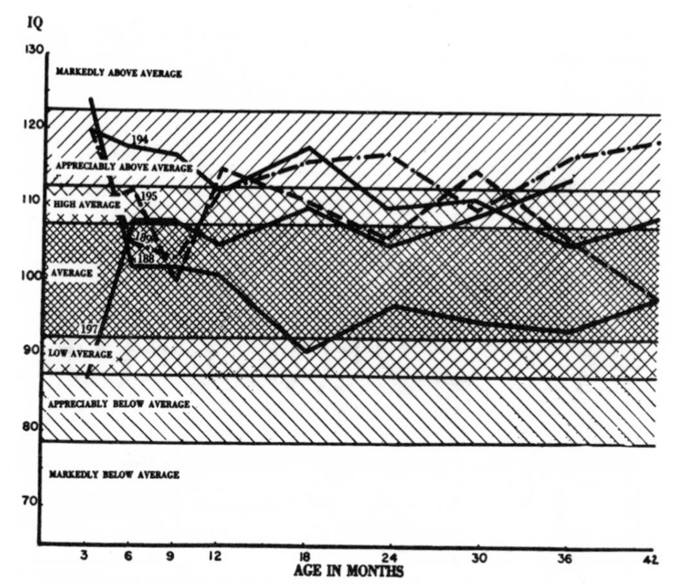

FIG. 5. Individual I.Q. curves of infants between the ages of three and forty-two months.

I.Q.'s obtained at thirty-six and forty-two months.

A study of the reliability and validity coefficients and of the individual I.Q. curves gives indications that the tests from about fifteen months on have nearly as high reliability and predictive value as do most intelligence tests for children of school age. For purposes of comparison the individual I.Q. curves of ten school children between the ages of six and eighteen years are plotted in Figures 9 and 10. These ten cases are a random selection taken from the Harvard Growth Study and made

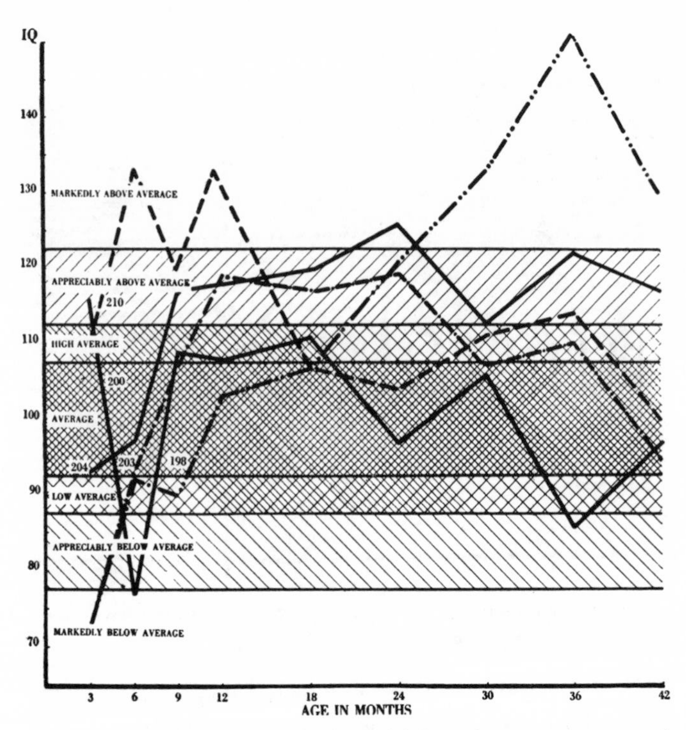

FIG. 6. Individual I.Q. curves of infants between the ages of three and forty-two months.

available to the writer through the kindness of Professor Walter F. Dearborn. At most of the ages the I.Q. plotted is the average of two well-known, standardized, group intelligence tests, but at the ages of six and seven only one test was given in most instances, and at two or three of the ages the I.Q.s obtained from three or more tests were averaged. Before the intelligence quotients

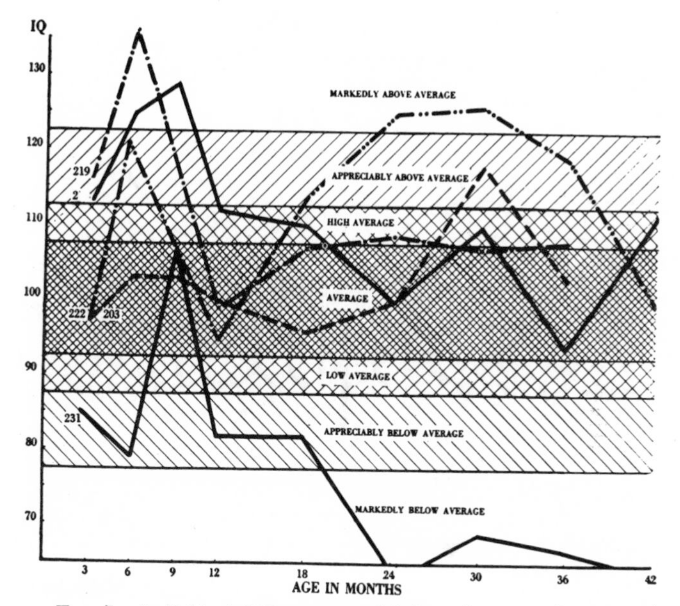

FIG. 7. Individual I.Q. curves of infants between the ages of three and forty-two months.

were averaged, each was equated to the Stanford-Binet (1916 Form). For a description of the tests used the reader is referred to "Data on the Growth of Public School Children" by Walter F. Dearborn and associates,[5] and for the method of equating to "Analysis of Results Obtained from Intelligence Tests and Examinations" by John M. Ratcliffe.[6]

[5] Walter F. Dearborn, John W. M. Rothney and Frank K. Shuttleworth: *Data on the Growth of Public School Children.* Monographs of the Society for Research in Child Development, Vol. III, No. 1. Washington, D. C. 1939.

[6] Unpublished Doctorate Thesis, Harvard University. 1934.

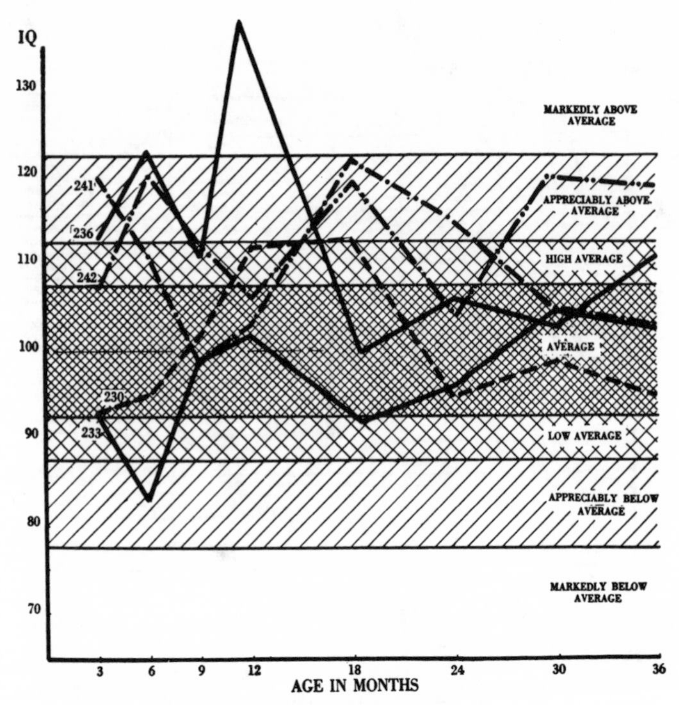

FIG. 8. Individual I.Q. curves of infants between the ages of three and thirty-six months.

A comparison of the I.Q. curves of the older children with those of the infants gives evidence pointing toward the conclusion that a single Infant Test given after the age of twelve or fifteen months gives an I.Q. that predicts future development about as adequately as that of the average of two of the better-known group intelligence tests given to school children, even when the group intelligence tests have been equated to a common

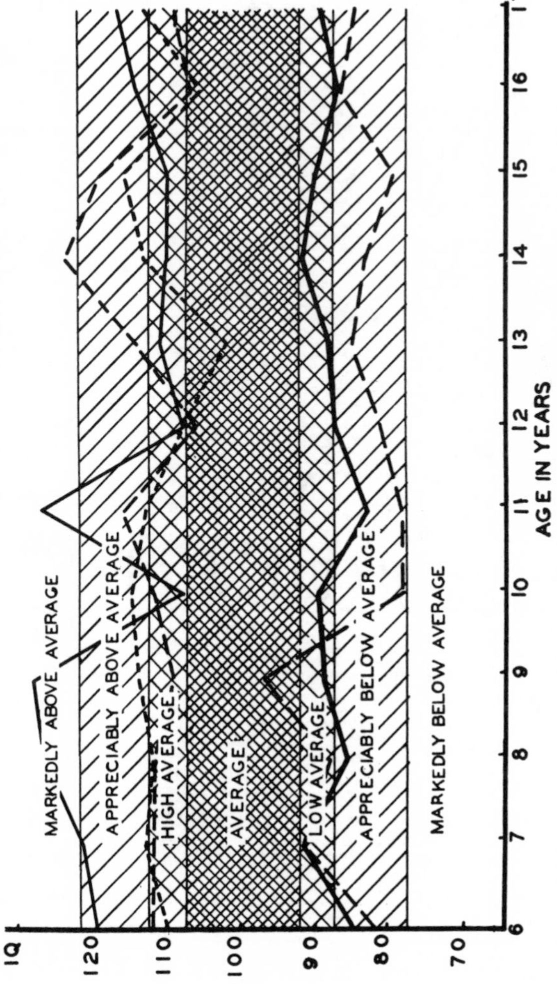

FIG. 9. I.Q. curves of individual school children between the ages of six and seventeen years.

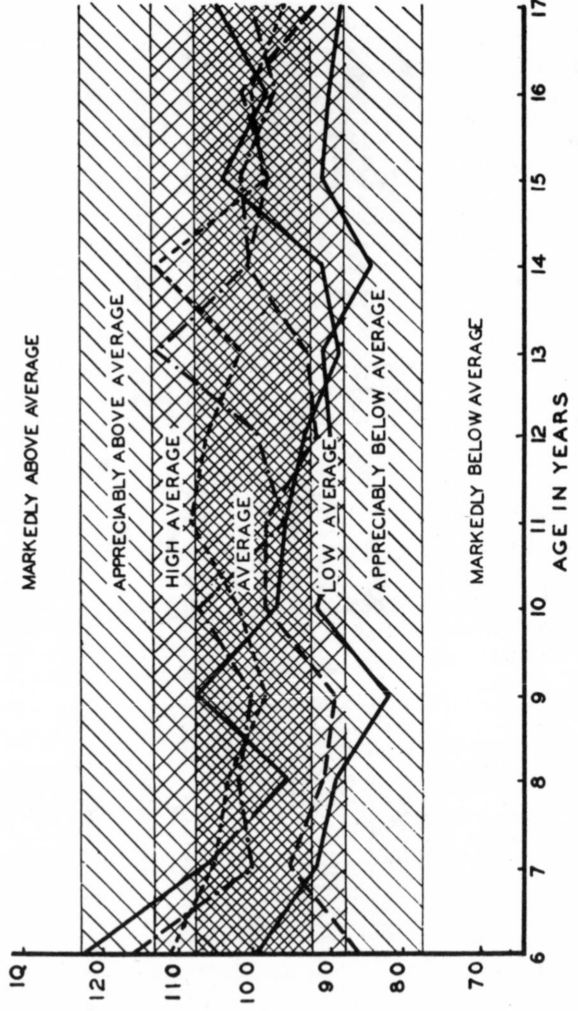

FIG. 10. I.Q. curves of individual school children between the ages of six and seventeen years.

standard. At twelve months the predictive value of the Infant Tests is appreciably less as is evidenced by a correlation coefficient of + 0.56 between them and the tests given at thirty-six months: below twelve months it is still less. Both the individual I.Q. curves and the correlation coefficients with later tests indicate that when the child is examined for purposes of predicting his future development little weight should be placed on the numerical rating alone when obtained before about fifteen months. In spite of their low predictive value these tests for the very young infant are often of value to the psychologist, experienced in the interpretation of infant behavior in the light of the infant's hereditary background and developmental history. Their greatest value is in alerting the psychologist to the possible extremes of brightness and retardation in cases of impending adoption and thus decreasing the danger of placing a child in a home where his intelligence will vary from that of the adopting parents to such an extent that, as he grows older, it may interfere with his successful adjustment in the home.

The infant who earns a score markedly above average, even as young as three or four months, has considerably better than average chances of possessing superior intelligence at school age. On the other hand the infant that tests low more often than not continues to develop slowly and has below average ability at school age. However, his chances of reaching the norm are greater than are the chances of the infant who tests markedly above average dropping below the norm. It is, therefore, evident that an infant should not be labeled unadoptable as the result of his performance on tests given during any brief period of time, but rather that all decisions regarding future plans for the infant who tests low should be postponed until further information can be obtained and the rate of his development determined.

For these reasons the test items for the early months were retained in the battery, but it is not recommended that they be used by the psychological examiner who has not had wide experience in the study of infant behavior and the interpretation of psychological test results in conjunction with other clinical data.

The emphasis that has been placed on the caution with which these intelligence tests should be used applies not only to these tests but to all tests for infants, and with only a little less force to those for children of preschool and school ages. There is no age from birth to maturity at which it is safe to base an important decision on the results of intelligence tests alone. The intelligence quotients obtained from these tests, as those from other intelligence tests, should always be interpreted in the light of other relevant information such as behavior during the examination, home environment, premature birth, serious illnesses, etc.

There is a growing body of data which points to the conclusion that part of the I.Q. variations resulting in lowered validity coefficients and the crossing and recrossing of growth curves is the result of changes in the tempo of development rather than the inadequacy of the tests. An example is Case 198 (Figure 11). This child had an obtained I.Q. of 73 at three months and one near 90 at both six and nine months. At one year and at each six-month interval thereafter up to the end of the third year she showed a comparatively steady gain. Between three and thirty-six months eight examinations were made, and, with one exception, where there was a decrease of two I.Q. points, each test resulted in a higher I.Q. than the previous test. The mother, a patrol policeman's wife, selected the child's college at the time of her birth. At twelve months the pediatrician who examined the baby regretted that the mother was probably doomed to disappointment. The pediatrician's prediction was in line with mental test ratings obtained at that time, but at three years the child's I.Q. was 150 and at four years she informed the examiner that she was animate but her

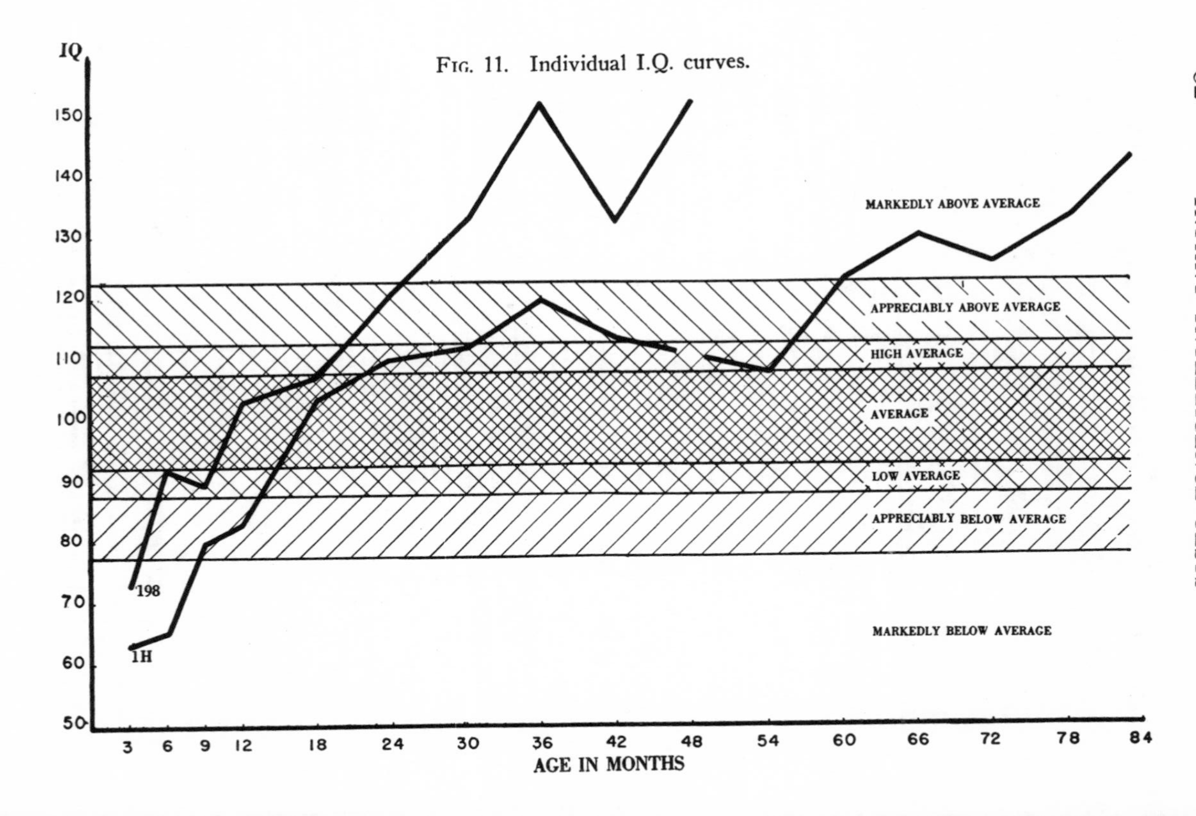

FIG. 11. Individual I.Q. curves.

doll was inanimate. This one case lowered the validity coefficients by twelve points at nine months and that for the other younger age groups by approximately the same amount. Case 1H, also shown in Figure 11, shows a somewhat similar rise in I.Q., though less regular and spread over a longer period. When but two or three tests are out of line the most probable cause may be an inadequate examination, but when seven successive tests show a consistent trend away from "constancy" this opinion cannot well be held. In these instances it appears more probable that the child's mental development was progressing at an increasingly rapid rate.

Another type of curve which appears to result from a temporary change in rate of growth, possibly as the result of a major physical or emotional disturbance, is shown in Case 202, Figure 12. This child missed his two-year examination on account of illness, at which time he lay near death for several weeks. The following three examinations at six-month intervals show a definite downward trend, indicating a slowing up of mental growth. The fourth examination shows a break in the downward trend and a slight upward turn and the fifth a definite gain, giving hope that the former rate of development may be regained.

Occasionally one finds an I.Q. curve that runs along comparatively horizontally and then shows

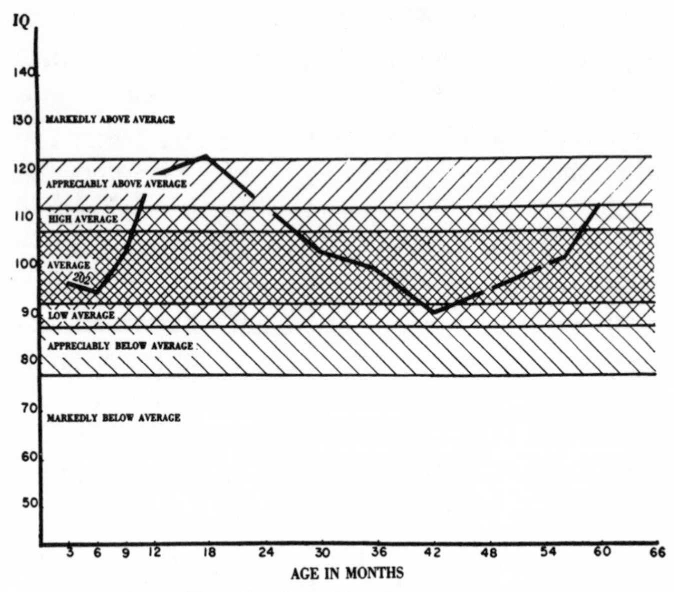

FIG. 12. Individual I.Q. curve.

a sudden drop or rise and the new level maintained for several successive semi-annual examinations. Cases 15 and 18, Figure 13, are examples in older children. Possibly school entrance may be a factor in these two cases.

The consistent trend of the curves makes it appear probable in these and in similar cases that the mental level of the child was adequately measured at the time, but that there were definite changes in the rate of mental development which caused later changes in the I.Q. Although such cases do not indicate that the test results lacked validity, they

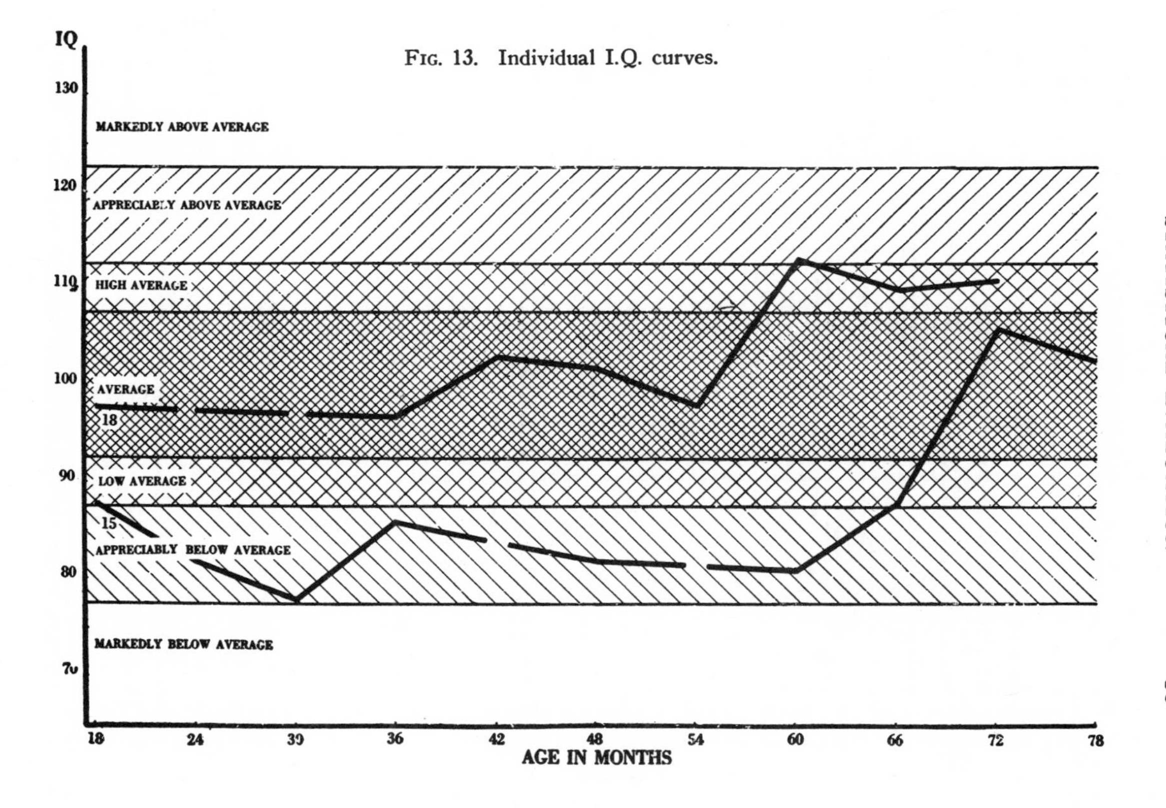

Fig. 13. Individual I.Q. curves.

do appreciably reduce the validity coefficients obtained by correlating earlier and later test results. If there were available some other reliable criteria of the intelligence of the child at the time the test was given with which to correlate the obtained mental ages, it is probable that the validity coefficients would be appreciably higher than those reported above.

Chapter III

GENERAL INSTRUCTIONS FOR ADMINISTERING INFANT TESTS

1. *Introduction:* The examining of infants and of children under two and one-half years of age for the purpose of estimating mental development is quite different from the examining of children of school age and is considerably more difficult. The small infant cannot understand verbal instructions, his attention span is short and he cannot be brought back to the task in hand by verbal requests. Even with two-year-olds, words can be depended upon only for the simplest requests such as "What's that?" "John do," "Where is . . .?" etc. The only instance in which slightly more complicated language may be used is when part of the purpose of the item is to test the child's language comprehension. The stage must be set so that the child of his own initiative will respond to the various test situations on a plane which is appropriate to his mental level. Great care has been taken in preparing this series of tests to select items to which the child will respond on as high a plane as his development will permit, provided that he is happy, wide awake and at ease. For example, when conditions are favorable a small infant placed face down on the table will, when he is not tired or sleepy, raise his head if he is able

to do so. A few weeks later he will also raise his chest, and as soon as development has made sufficient progress he will use his arms to assist in his chest-raising. When a baby first attempts to pick up a small pellet, he uses a whole-hand movement in which he attempts to rake the pellet against his palm with his fingers. As development proceeds he will use his thumb and finger to secure the pellet and, having once acquired this higher form of behavior, he seldom goes back to the more primitive form of grasp. If a cup and a pile of small cubes are placed before the seven-month-old child, his attention will shift from one cube to another or from a cube to the cup. He does not play with them in combination until the age of nine or ten months has been reached, at which time he may be expected to hit the cup and cube together, or perhaps place his hand with the cube in the cup. but he probably[1] will not release his grasp on the cube while it is in the cup until his mental development has reached the level of eleven or twelve months. By seventeen months the typical response is to continue picking up one cube after another and placing them in the cup until the task is completed.

2. *The Examiner:* The examiner should have a

[1] Such words as "usually" and "probably," etc., that appear throughout this chapter are used advisedly. It will be clear to all who are familiar with standardized test procedures that while a mean response of a given group may be typical, individual variations are always present. If this were not so only one intelligence test item would be needed at each age level.

sound background in child psychology, including the mental testing of school children. This, combined with a nursery school training course, is an ideal background for the student who is planning to prepare himself for the testing of infants and preschool-age children. No student who has not acquired, in one way or another, skill in handling small children should attempt to give psychological examinations to them. No amount of general or specific knowledge will make an examiner successful if he is unable to adapt himself to the personality and mood of the child and to treat the child as an individual worthy of respect. However, it is not intended to imply that everyone who is familiar with children can adequately qualify for administering the tests and interpreting the results through the study of the directions given herewith. The usual training of a teacher or nurse, for example, would not give an adequate background for so doing. Only the person who has had a thorough training in child psychology, including experience in psychometric procedures, should attempt to master the techniques described below without the supervision of a well-qualified psychologist.

The attitude and maner of the examiner should be quiet, friendly and matter of fact; his voice quiet and low, and his speech slow and distinct.

3. *The Room and Its Furnishings:* The examination should be conducted in a quiet, light, well-

ventilated room furnished plainly but with a homelike comfortable appearance. It should bear no resemblance to a hospital room or a doctor's office, which might remind the child of past unhappy experiences. Two or three simple pictures on the wall sometimes serve to start the small child talking. If they are simple pictures of a cat, dog, automobile, bird, etc., they may serve to stimulate the year-old baby to speak spontaneously his only word. They do not hold the child's interest sufficiently long to interfere with the examination. One toy selected to attract immediate interest and which may be used as an introduction to the test materials should be on the table when the child enters the room. No other toys or distracting visual stimuli should be in sight, and the room should be free from distracting sounds. A continuous babble of talking and laughter in a nearby room or the rumble of traffic is usually less distracting than periodic unexpected noises, such as persons passing by the door at intervals, or of a truck or fire engine in the street below. Perfect testing conditions cannot always be attained, but the examiner can usually find a satisfactory room available and should insist on this and otherwise suitable conditions before undertaking to administer the tests. Standardized tests given under adverse conditions, or without standard procedures, are so unreliable that the results are likely to be more harmful than helpful in influencing diagnosis and if frequently repeated would soon throw the tests into discredit.

The child should be made as comfortable as possible, either seated at or lying on a table. He should be kept out of drafts, light should not shine in his eyes, and over-tight clothing should be loosened. If he is to sit on a chair by himself it is immaterial in so far as the child is concerned whether the table is high or low, provided that his elbows are approximately on the level with the table and that he has a satisfactory foot rest. A higher table is more comfortable for the examiner and is just as satisfactory for the child. Arms on the chair discourage the child from getting up and walking away, yet do not appear to cause him to feel restrained. A chair and table high enough so that the child's feet are above the floor act as a further deterent to an impulse to move off. Most children are used to sitting in a high chair, and unless they have been in nursery school are likely to be more at home in one than when sitting on a low chair at a low table. A rim around three sides of the table about one-quarter of an inch in height is a great help in preventing objects from rolling or being pushed to the floor. The table found entirely satisfactory in the standardization of these tests was 25 inches high with a top 24 by 32 inches, having a quarter-inch rim around the edge on three sides. The chairs for the examiner and the attendant who holds the child were 14 inches high. These height measurements were obtained by cutting three inches from the legs of a table and chairs of standard height. They were found to be reasonably comfortable for the examiner and much more comfortable for the attendant who holds the child and for the child sitting on her lap than was a chair and table of standard height. On a higher chair the short or stout woman usually had difficulty in keeping her lap flat and the child was constantly sliding toward the floor. On the low chair this difficulty is not encountered and the tall woman can keep her lap flat by stretching her feet forward or back.

A table 25 inches high and a chair of standard height (17 inches) with arms and an adjustable foot rest is satisfactory for the child who sits alone. The height of the seat may be adjusted by means of flat pillows. For those tests that are given in a lying position, a thick, soft but firm pad should be placed on the table and covered with a waterproof sheet over which may be placed a white sheet of either cloth or paper. A heavy blanket folded the size of the table makes a satisfactory pad.

4. *The Mother:* There is disagreement among psychologists as to whether or not the mother or other attendant should be allowed in the room during an examination. Some maintain that she should never be allowed in the room; others are of the opinion that the child responds more readily in her presence, while still others would only allow

her to be present if the child is shy. If the child is shy when he first enters the room, as is usually the case between the ages of 15 and 30 months, and if the rating must be obtained at the first visit, we have found that the chances of a successful examination are greater with the mother present. It is desirable to explain to the mother before the examination what is expected of her and of the child. She should be told that the examiner wishes to see what the child will do without any help or criticism from her; that later the examiner will wish to see what the child will do for his mother, if there is reason to believe that he might respond differently for her. The mother is much less likely to become agitated if she has been told that the child is not expected to give correct responses to all the items of the test. Such an explanation tactfully made will also usually prevent the mother from urging, scolding or otherwise interfering with the examination and will prevent her from thinking that her knowledge of the child is not taken seriously. The mother should sit where the child cannot see her face too readily. When the child is under two and one-half years this is easily arranged by having him sit on her lap. When the child is older the mother should sit beside and slightly behind him. If she can be interested in reading a magazine so much the better. A child of two and one-half years or under will usually overcome his shyness more quickly and sit longer without becoming restless when on his mother's lap than when on a chair alone.

5. *The Child:* If reliable results are to be obtained, the child must not be sick, tired, sleepy, or in an antagonistic or unhappy mood at the time of examination. He should be at ease and on friendly, cooperative terms with the examiner. If these conditions cannot be attained during the first ten or fifteen minutes in the examining room, it is best to postpone the examination until another day. At times it is obvious that a child is not feeling up to par or is too unhappy, antagonistic or ill at ease to do his best, but at other times it is very difficult to detect these and other unsatisfactory conditions within the child.

6. *Approach to the Child and Maintenance of Rapport:* In all individual intelligence testing it is of paramount importance that friendly cooperative relations between the examiner and the examinee be developed and maintained throughout the examination period. Barring the first few months of life, the younger the child the more important and the more difficult this becomes. The infant's or small child's confidence cannot be gained by verbal explanations, but must be built up through an easy confident, friendly manner. It is very seldom that the examiner should at any time show disapproval of the child's actions or give him any inkling that he has made an unsatisfactory response. A single "no-no" accompanied by a slight frown will occasionally make impossible

the successful completion of an examination of a sensitive child. The examiner must be ever alert to note the first indications of fatigue or boredom and be ready to counteract them with appropriate praise, encouragement or quick surprise presentations of new toys, etc. A few children below the age of two years are afraid to pick up the toys placed before them. Sometimes this is the result of fear of new or strange objects, but it is more often the result of having been frequently told at home not to touch this and that, and perhaps receiving a slap or harsh words for forgetfulness. In either case friendly, tactful urging will usually overcome the child's resistance.

When the child enters the room he should be given a friendly smile and a brief, casual, verbal greeting. Care must be taken not to appear too serious or aggressive or to look at him too intently. If he withdraws or shows other evidence of shyness, it is usually best for the examiner to immediately turn his attention from the child and a moment later offer a toy with a smile and a brief glance. A quiet low voice and rather slow speech is liked by children in general and will go a long way toward reassuring an infant or shy child. At times a child who enters the room sobbing or screaming and kicking will quickly forget his shyness or antagonism if his crying is entirely ignored and if he is treated almost in the same manner as he would have been if he had entered the room in a more favorable mood.

An introductory toy that has a strong immediate appeal but which does not stimulate prolonged interest should be on the table when the child enters the room and be pushed toward him as soon as he is seated. A doll, automobile or ball are not good objects as the child's interest in them is likely to be prolonged and he is frequently unwilling to exchange them for the test materials. As the examination proceeds the child is quick to learn that when one toy is removed another will appear and in his eagerness to investigate the new toy he is ready to give up the old. Some toy which sets a definite objective task for the child which can be completed in a short time is the ideal introductory toy. For children who have reached the age of 18 months a peg or form board serves the purpose well. Almost all children are interested in them and after they have placed the pegs or forms they have a feeling of having completed a task and are ready to exchange them for another toy which usually may be the first item of the test. The introductory task must, of course, be appropriate to the child's ability. It should be simple enough to insure success, but difficult enough to arouse the child's interest. The examiner should keep extra toys of a similar type handy so that they may be presented if the child is not yet ready to continue with the test proper. If the child fails to take an immediate interest in the first toy he may be tactfully urged to perform the task set by the object, but this should be dropped and another toy taken up before the coaxing has reached the point of disturbing the child emotionally and arousing further shyness or antagonism.

The desirable amount of free talking interspersed between the set speeches will depend upon the child. Some will respond most satisfactorily with practically none, while others do better with an almost continual stream of comments. In so far as possible the "extra" conversation should be confined to the periods between the completion of one item and the presentation of the next, at which time there is but little danger of invalidating the child's responses. Any other talking by the examiner must be so worded that it will neither increase nor decrease the likelihood of a successful response. The words used should be the simplest possible, but one should not talk down to the child. Except for a few words "baby talk" should never be used unless it is known that the mother of the child uses a special word for a particular object. The words "choo-choo" for train, "bow-wow" for dog, "tick-tock" for clock and "kitty" for cat are so commonly used with small children that they should be used if the child does not respond to the correct word. Also some children respond to certain nouns more readily if an "ie" is added to them as "doggie," "horsie," "birdie," etc. In most instances the child of two and a half or younger has been talked to by only a few persons and sometimes very little by these. Unless the examiner speaks slowly and distinctly the child may not recognize words that are spoken in a different voice and with a slightly different enunciation from that of his mother.

7. *Importance of Following Standardized Procedure:* It is of the greatest importance that the standardized procedures for giving and scoring the tests be followed exactly. They were carefully formulated and tried out on large numbers of children. Many were tried out in several forms before the most satisfactory one was selected. The reason for following the procedures described, however, is not that they are necessarily better than others that might be devised, but is that the tests have been standardized on these procedures and if others are substituted, the results obtained probably would not be comparable with the norms. The set speeches for the examiner's use in testing children of these ages are of necessity short and few in number. There should be no difficulty in memorizing them along with the methods for presenting the materials to the child. The emphasis laid on following the directions does not mean that the examination must be conducted in a stiff or formal manner. On the contrary, the examiner should become so familiar with the procedures that he can give his whole attention to following the set directions in a natural spontaneous manner. Although the directions require very little speech, there should be enough additional talking to give a free, friendly atmosphere. Any conversation beyond the set speeches should be of

a non-committal type, carefully worded to make sure that the difficulty of the item is not affected. If at any time it should become necessary to deviate from the prescribed procedures, detailed notes of the facts should be recorded where they will be seen by anyone who may use the test results, and if possible an alternate item should be used in scoring the test. All items requiring verbal responses should be recorded verbatim. This is a comparatively easy task with very young children as they are almost always brief. Any unusual responses to the non-verbal items, whether good or poor, should be described; also any comments made by the mother which might assist in interpreting the test results.

8. *Interviewing Parents:* When it is necessary to obtain information through questioning the parent or attendant rather than through direct observation greater accuracy may be attained if questions that can be answered by "yes" or "no" or other single words are avoided or supplemented by additional questions. Examples or descriptions of the activity in question should be obtained. A parent's understanding of certain terms such as "combines words" may be quite different from the standard required by the test.

9. *Order of Presentation of Items:* No definite order of presentation of items has been set, since the best results with small children are obtained by varying the order according to the interests of the child. If the child is six months of age or under,

it is usually best to give first those items which are administered in a lying position. He is less likely to protest at being laid down when he first enters the room than he is after he has been allowed to sit up. Up to and including the five-month tests some of the items are given in the lying position and some sitting. From six months on all are given in the latter position. The position to be used is stated in the directions up to the sixth month.

The first two or three items should usually be those which will probably have the greatest appeal. As soon as interest has been thoroughly aroused it is well to give some item that is scored at several levels such as the picture vocabulary or pointing to pictures, which will give an idea of the child's general level of mental development. The examiner must be ever alert to take advantage of the child's interest and curiosity, and to present each item at the most favorable moment. If the child indicates a desire to take the examiner's pencil, this is the time to give a paper and pencil test, if he is attracted by a particular box, this is the time to give the item contained in that box, etc. No object that the child would not be allowed to play with if he so desired should be within the range of his vision. The items that are likely to be of less interest should be given after he has become well adjusted to the situation, but before he has had an opportunity to become tired or restless, and they should be interspersed between items of greater appeal. For example, if a child should happen to have little interest in the cubes but be eager to manipulate other objects, he should not be given two cube tests in succession, but should be given some other items such as beads and box, pellet and bottle, pencil and paper, etc., between them. If the child should become bored with building the tower, it is permissible to sandwich another test between the trials should that seem desirable. One may even go so far as to gently rattle a *closed* box and say "Now make another and then we will see what is in this box." However, there is seldom any need to resort to bribery in order to obtain cooperation. When an item is refused by the child or is spoiled in the process of giving an alternate item should be substituted.

10. *Time Limits:* No time limit has been set for the tests as a whole or for the individual items. In general, time limits in a test for preschool children are undesirable. Any suggestion of hurrying usually affects the speed of the older preschool child adversely and is not comprehended at all by the younger child. In a timed test the bright child is often penalized by his talkativeness and his fertile imagination. He sees a pegboard as a boat with smoke stacks and starts pushing it over the table before all the pegs are placed; or the toy cat reminds him of the kitten at home and he must tell the examiner about it before he will complete the task in hand. This situation arises more frequently among the bright than among the dull

children. Another type of child that is unjustly penalized by a timed test is the slow, deliberate but at times highly intelligent child. He stops to think before he acts and may give an unusually large number of correct responses, but in many of them he is likely to exceed the time required by the average child.

While no time limits are set it is important that the examination proceed as rapidly as may be compatible with an atmosphere of calm leisure which is so important in dealing with infants and young children. For the small baby the examination takes from 20 to 30 minutes and for the older child the average time is approximately 30 minutes. The skilled examiner can keep the majority of children interested and happy for this length of time without any difficulty, but there are a few children whose interest span is short and every minute that can be cut from the testing time is well worth whatever effort it may cost.

The examiner should have the test material out of sight, either behind a screen or in closed boxes and it should be so arranged that he can instantly put his hand on any desired piece of material without fumbling. He should form the habit of presenting one set of materials with one hand while removing with the other that with which the child has just finished. This not only reduces the total examination period appreciably but also decreases the likelihood of boredom or restlessness on the part of the child or of his protesting at the removal of an attractive toy. One minute of waiting will contribute appreciably more toward the child becoming fatigued than the same amount of time spent in working on the test items. Of course, no child should be expected to sit at a single task for thirty minutes, but the examination is so arranged that one interesting occupation follows another in quick succession. Before the child has had time to tire of one task he finds another before him. The time spent on each individual item of the test averages about one minute.

11. *Range of the Examination:* The testing should begin with items that are likely to arouse the child's interest and give him an opportunity to achieve success. It should extend downward until the items have become so easy that all five of one age level have been passed and upward until a level is reached at which all five are failed. Slightly greater accuracy may be attained by continuing downward until all the items at two successive age levels have been passed and upward until all at two levels have been failed. The slight increase in accuracy gained, however, does not ordinarily justify the extra time required, except on rare occasions when there is some reason to suspect that the full range of the child's development has not been sampled.

12. *Scoring Individual Test Items:* There have been occasional reports indicating that the norms are based on a below average sample of the population. That is, that the rating obtained on the

infant tests are not maintained but drop when the child is later examined with the Stanford-Binet or other standardized tests. In some instances at least this has been due to a tendency for the examiner to be too liberal in giving the child the "benefit of the doubt." There are a number of items in the test where it is possible for the infant to make an apparently "plus" response by chance. Before credit is given for such an item the examiner must determine whether or not the child's response was purposeful or the result of random play. Repetition and careful observation is often necessary before an item can be scored. A few examples are given below.

In testing the infant's response to the sound of the voice or the bell care must be taken to avoid the possibility of the baby responding to a shadow rather than the sound.

In item 4 at eight months the pellet often sticks to a baby's moist hand. Before credit is given it must be established that the pellet has actually been grasped between the fingers and the palm.

Item 3 at nine months is one of the most difficult to score. If the bell is waved or banged on the table in exactly the same manner as the spoon, ring or other objects credit cannot be given for imitating the ringing of the bell.

When the child pulls the ring toward him by means of the string the examiner must make sure that the string has been pulled with the purpose of obtaining the ring before credit is given. If the ring is drawn forward when the baby is merely manipulating the string and he pays no attention to the ring until he sees it move, credit cannot be given.

Credit cannot be given for "adjusts to gesture" because the proud mother has seen the baby clapping his hands together in play. Before credit is given it must be established that he plays "Pat-a-cake" or some other activity in immediate imitation of a demonstration.

Other examples could be given. In general the examiner must be ever alert to determine whether the responses to the items are purposeful or whether the correct response has been hit upon by chance during random play. In the latter case credit must not be given.

The examiner must also be cautious in scoring an item refused. It is difficult to distinguish between a refusal and inability to respond to the item. It is, however, seldom that a baby who is rested, wide awake and not shy will not respond to the test items in an appropriate manner if he is able to do so. For example if the baby takes the first cube and fails to approach the second, or if he takes the second and fails to approach the third the item must be scored minus rather than a refusal. The reason for his lack of interest is probably lack of maturity. If a baby is brought in for an examination when he is tired, sleepy or shy he should be given a period of play and if within five or ten minutes he has not overcome these conditions the examination should be postponed until some future time. Several sittings are occasionally required before a baby gets over his shyness sufficiently for a satisfactory test to be administered.

13. *Scoring:* The principle of scoring is the same as for the Stanford-Binet. The groups of different levels of difficulty are, however, closer together and contain five instead of six items which make different weighting necessary. All items are scored either plus or minus. No half credits are given. Each age level through two and one-half years contains five items. The credit given for each item passed is, therefore, one fifth of the interval covered by the series of tests of the level of difficulty in question. As in the Stanford-Binet, the tests at each level cover the preceding period of mental development. For example, the items at the twelve months level cover the period from eleven to twelve months, those at twenty-seven months cover the period from twenty-four to twenty-seven months, etc. The age interval covered by the groups of items from two to twelve months is one month, so that each item passed is given a credit of .2 months. From 14 to 24 months inclusive each group of items covers a two-month interval so that each item is given a credit of .4 of a month. For the age groups 27 and 30 months, the interval is three months and the credit for each item is .6 of a month. If the child passes any item at the thirty-month level he is given the New Revised Stanford-Binet test of intelligence, Form L, beginning at

three years. The materials, procedures and scoring described by Terman and Merrill in *Measuring Intelligence*[2] are used. For each item passed up to and including five years one additional month credit is given.

Example of Scoring: If a child passed all the items at the ten-month level, four at eleven months, two at twelve months, three at fourteen months, one at sixteen months and none at eighteen months, his score would be as follows:

Basal age	10.0
Credit for 11-month items	.8
" " 12 " "	.4
" " 14 " "	1.2
" " 16 " "	.4
" " 18 " "	0
Mental age	12.8 months

14. *Importance of Accuracy in Recording and Calculating Derived Scores:* Reading over the notes made, checking the birth dates, calculations, etc., should be made a routine part of the test procedure. Mistakes are common in reporting chronological ages. The mother's statement of the date of birth should never be accepted without verification. Errors occur in the reports of persons of all ages and all economic levels. The author once made a bet with a co-worker that among two hundred normal school girls there would be at least four errors among the dates of birth which they

[2] Boston: Houghton Mifflin. 1937.

reported. Eleven errors were found. Aside from the accidental errors it is not uncommon for a parent purposely to report a false birth date in order to get his child entered in school before the legal age or in the hope of making a dull child appear brighter. Another common source of error is found in the arithmetical processes required in calculating the chronological age and the intelligence quotient. All calculations should be carefully checked as should the whole scoring process. Any arithmetic that may be required should be recorded directly on the examination blank where it may readily be re-checked at a later date should occasion arise.

The examiner should always go over the blank immediately after giving an examination to make sure that the notes and comments are full, legible and that they will be understandable to other psychologists who may have occasion to refer to the test blank at a later date. The examiner frequently scribbles down valuable bits of descriptive information, but because he is at the same time observing the child, the handwriting may be so illegible that even he would be unable to read it after the lapse ot a few months. If he goes over the blank after the examination, he can make sure that his notes are clear and complete, and transcribe any personal shorthand that may have been used during the examination.

15. *Use of Test Results:* Great care must be used in the interpretation of the test results. If

there is an important decision to be made, the examiner should insist on a second examination, preferably after several weeks, to be followed by a third, six months to a year later. The purpose of repeating the examinations at short intervals is to check on the accuracy of the results, whereas the purpose of the long intervals is to determine whether the child is gaining or losing relative to his age. This is especially important after serious illness. If the results of two tests are not in agreement, or, if there is any contradictory evidence such as the child's action at home or at nursery school or in his developmental history, diagnosis should be postponed until further examination can be made.

After a sufficient amount of experience an examiner often has a "feeling" that the child is not working up to his capacity but he may be unable to put a finger on the reasons for the "hunch." Such notes as the following may be found in the records of the present study: "Seemed to be happy and to feel at home but did not appear to be doing his best," "I.Q. 83 but appeared entirely normal," and, more obvious, "The child had just been through the orthopedic and x-ray examinations; he appeared tired, was fussy and refused a few items; probably did not do his best." Judging from earlier and later examinations on the same child, it was found that these clinical observations were correct in about one-half the instances in which they were at variance with the test score. This means that the observations of the examiner made during the examination but not required for the actual scoring of the test may be of the utmost importance. Whenever they are in contradiction to the test score the results must be interpreted with special caution, especially if they are to be passed on to others interested in the child.

If the standardized procedures of administering and scoring the tests are followed, the examiner will find that his objective test results are much more reliable than his subjective opinion, but as experience accumulates, the subjective clinical impression will become more and more valuable. Instances in which there are conflicting results between the adequately administered test and the subjective opinion of a well-trained psychologist are the exceptions, but occasionally the exception is important.

After an examination one should always review the test and form an opinion as to whether or not the final rating seems to fit the child. If there appears to be any discrepancy between the child's behavior and his score, the test blank should be carefully checked for error and if no errors are found the discrepancy should be noted on the blank.

It is ordinarily unwise to report the intelligence test results to the parent and practically never should the I.Q. be stated. There are a number of reasons for this. The examiner must remember that there are a large number of factors which may contribute toward invalidating the test results and that any worry or elation of the parent resulting from the report may be based on false information. Aside from the unreliability of the individual test scores, there may be an actual change in the rate of mental growth resulting in an increase or decrease in I.Q. It is not as yet known what the chances are of the bright infant or preschool child maintaining his high standing, or what percentage of the dull children gain. It is known that the bright child of two is far more likely to be bright at ten than is the child who tests as dull or average at two, but how great these chances are for any one individual cannot be said with assurance. There are a few instances on record where there has been an extreme change in the child's relative mental level. (See Figures 11 to 13.) Aside from the above reasons only the exceptional parent has the background required for interpreting the results of the tests. Further one does not know what the terms used in describing the results will mean to the parent. There is always danger of the child being "labeled" by his neighbors and playmates. The mother is likely to tell her "best friend" and from there it may go far. A lot of envy, nagging, boasting and worry can be prevented by merely stating that the policy of the school or clinic is not to give out the results unless there is reason to believe that the knowledge will help in the treatment of the child at home.

16. *Summary:* No better summary of the requirements for valid intelligence test results can be given than the quotation below, taken from Terman and Merrill's instructions for giving the Stanford Revision of the Binet-Simon Intelligence Scale. It was written in connection with a test for older children but applies with equal force to the testing of children under two years of age:

> In order to secure a valid result . . . three requirements must be satisfied: (1) the standard procedures must be followed; (2) the child's best efforts must be enlisted by the establishment and maintenance of adequate rapport; and (3) the responses must be correctly scored. It can hardly be said that any one of the three is more important than the other, for all are absolutely essential. Unless the tests are given in strict accordance with the procedures by which they were standardized, the examiner can never be sure what his results mean. If he has failed to enlist the subject's best efforts, the only thing certain is that the resulting score will be too low in some unknown degree. Unless he has learned to score the responses according to the rules which have been laid down, his data will not be comparable to the norms.

CHAPTER IV

INSTRUCTIONS FOR GIVING AND SCORING THE TESTS

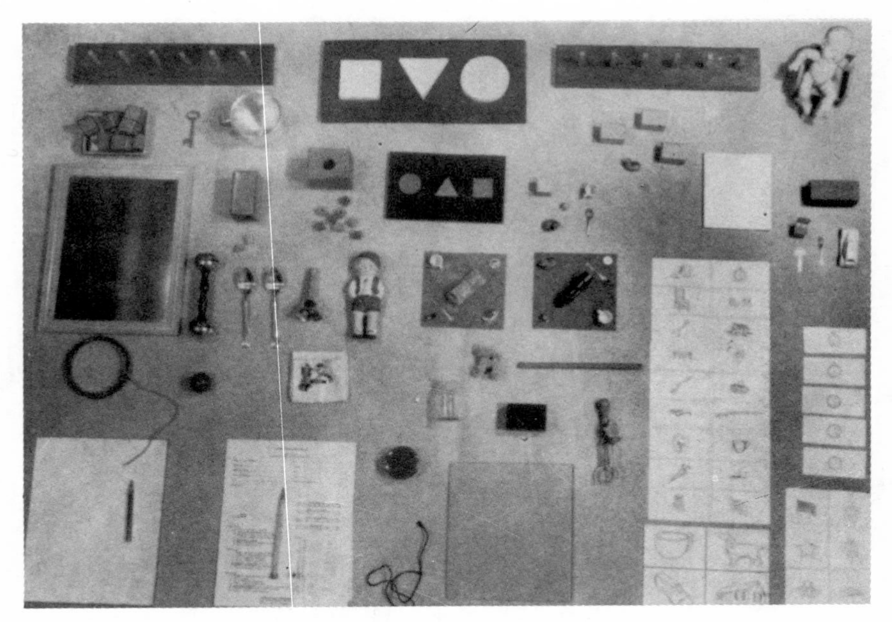

Complete set of material for administering the infant tests.

The materials and examination forms used in connection with the infant tests may be obtained from The Psychological Corporation, 522 Fifth Avenue, New York, N. Y. The material is put up in a convenient carrying case about the size and shape of a small suit case. They are so arranged in the case that they need not be unpacked and repacked every time the tests must be carried from one place to another. The examiner first places the case on a low table or chair to his left, turned so that the open cover shields the contents of the case from the child's vision. The large form board and box containing the mirror, pads of paper, cards and other large flat objects are merely lifted from the case and the two peg boards which are under the box stood on end in the back right hand corner of the case. Then the box is replaced in an upright position in the space that was formerly occupied by the peg boards, and the large form board is stood on end behind the mirror. The apparatus is now ready for use with every object, or the box in which it is contained, where it can be readily seen by the examiner. With a little practice the examiner can readily learn to slip each piece of material back in place as soon as he is through with it. He can then quickly lay his hands on it when it is next needed. When he is through examining, the material is packed for carrying merely by removing the large form board, lifting the box containing the mirror, laying the peg boards flat, then placing the box with the mirror, etc., face down and laying the large form board on top. The case is then ready to close.

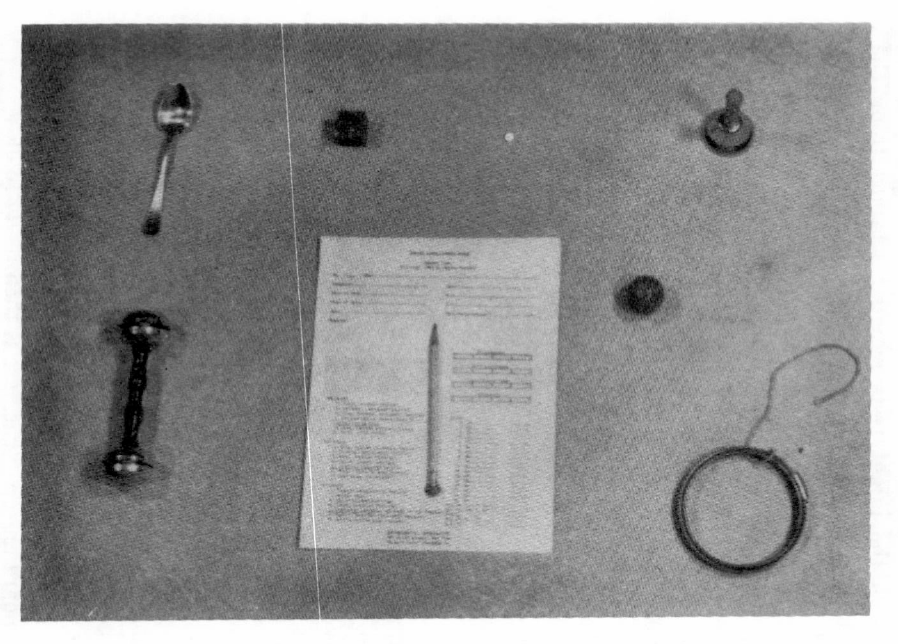

Test materials for ages two to five months inclusive.

2 Months

1. Attends to Voice

Procedure: The child is placed in a comfortable supine position. The examiner then leans over until his face is approximately ten inches from that of the child and talks to him in a quiet voice, smiling as he does so.

Scoring: Credit is given if the child gives evidence of listening.

2 Months

2. Inspects Environment

Procedure: It should be determined whether or not the child, when lying contentedly on his back, turns his eyes to look around the room, also if he turns his head in looking. The mother, in response to appropriate questions, can usually give a correct report. More reliable results are attained when the information can be obtained through direct observation, but the fact that the baby does not look around the room during the examination is not sufficient evidence that he has not learned to do so.

Scoring: Credit is given if the child investigates his environment visually with or without turning his head.

2 Months

3. Follows Ring in Horizontal Motion

Material: A four-inch wooden embroidery ring painted bright red with a string 15 inches in length attached.

Procedure: The embroidery ring is suspended by the string, about eight inches from the child's eyes while he is lying on his back. The ring should be moved about in different directions to attract attention. If his attention can be caught by the ring, it is moved in a horizontal arc about eight inches from his eyes at the rate of about five seconds to an arc. Next the ring is moved in a vertical arc in relation to the line of vision and then in a circle. It should be noted whether the child's eyes follow the moving ring in a continuous or in a transient manner or not at all; and whether or not there is increased activity of the arms or legs.

Scoring: Credit is given if the child's eyes follow the ring continuously as it is moved in a horizontal arc. (The first alternate item is also credited if he follows the ring when it is moved in a vertical arc; and he is given credit at three months if he follows it as it is moved in a circle.)

2 Months

4. Follows Moving Person

Procedure: As the child is lying on his back the examiner walks back and forth within easy view, either at the foot of the examining table or, if the child has a tendency to turn his head to one side, in whatever position is most directly in the child's line of vision.

Scoring: Credit is given if the child follows the examiner or other moving person with his eyes.

2 Months

5. Babbles

Procedure: The examiner leans over the child when he is lying on his back, until his face is about ten inches from that of the child, and talks to him in a low, quiet voice. If the child does not "talk" back it must be determined from the mother or attendant whether or not the child makes vocal sounds in play when alone or when he is talked to. An intelligent mother's report may ordinarily be relied upon. One is more likely to obtain a reliable report if questions that can be answered with a "yes" or "no" are avoided or are supplemented by other questions. Thus if it is stated that the child does babble, the mother may be asked, "How often?" and "On what occasions?" or "When?" If the mother is at a loss for an answer several possibilities may be given as: "When he first wakes?" "When he is played with?" "When he is alone?" etc.

Scoring: Credit is given if the child makes cooing or other vocal sounds.

2 Months

Alternate a. Follows Ring in Vertical Motion

Material: Embroidery ring. (See page 99.)

Procedure: The embroidery ring is suspended by a string, about eight inches from the child's eyes while he is lying on his back. It should be moved about in different directions to attract attention. If his attention can be caught by the ring, it is moved in a horizontal arc about eight inches from his eyes at the rate of about five seconds to an arc. Next the ring is moved vertically in relation to the eyes and then in a circle.

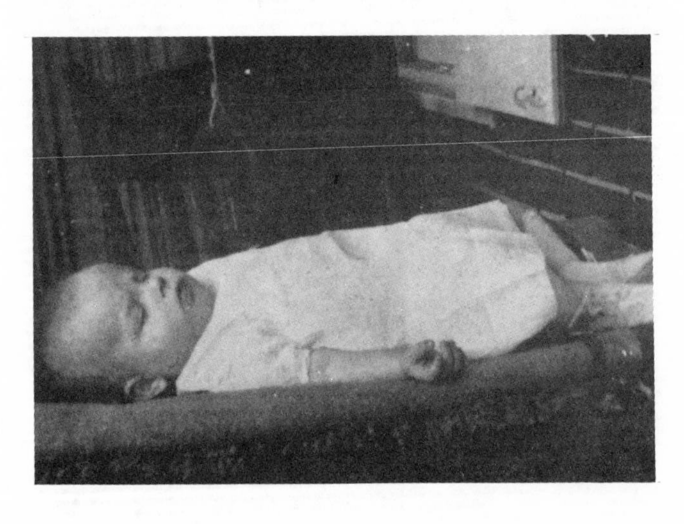

It should be noted whether the child's eyes follow the moving ring in a continuous or in a transient manner or not at all; and whether there is increased activity of the arms or legs.

Scoring: Credit is given if the child keeps his eyes fixed on the ring as it is moved back and forth vertically. (Credit is given for Item 3 at this age if he follows the ring as it is moved from side to side and at three months if he follows it when it is moved in a circle.)

2 Months

Alternate b. LIFTS HEAD IN PRONE POSITION

Procedure: The child is laid face down on a soft but firm surface.

Scoring: Credit is given if the child raises his head from the table and holds it up for several seconds. (He is also given credit at three months if he raises his chest from the table and supports it by means of his arms.)

3 Months

1. Follows Ring in Circular Motion

Material: Embroidery ring. (See page 99.)

Procedure: The embroidery ring is suspended by a string, about eight inches from the child's eyes while he is lying on his back. It should be moved about in different directions to attract attention. If his attention can be caught by the ring, it is moved in a horizontal arc about eight inches from his eyes at the rate of about five seconds to an arc. Next the ring is moved vertically in relation to the eyes and then in a circle. It should be noted whether the child's eyes follow the moving ring in a continuous or

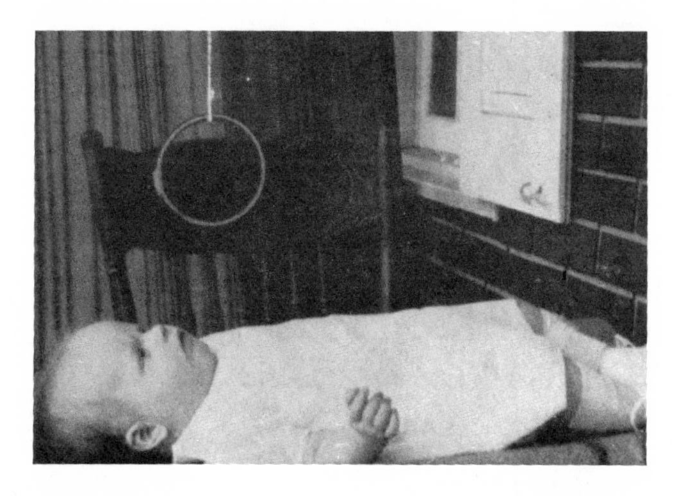

in a transient manner and whether there is increased activity of the arms or legs.

Scoring: Credit is given if the ring is followed continuously as it is moved in a circle. (Credit is given at two months if he follows the ring when it is moved in a horizontal or vertical arc and at four months if there is increased activity of the arms and legs.)

3 Months

2. Anticipates Feeding

Procedure: Unless the child is being examined at feeding time, the examiner must depend on the report of the mother or attendant for the required information. In most cases the question "When the child sees the bottle do you think that he knows he is going to be fed?" brings a definite answer from the mother. But if she should merely answer "Yes" then she should be asked what the child does to make her think that he knows he is going to be fed. If the child is entirely breast fed or if he has not been given at least two bottles of milk a day for at least two weeks, this item must be omitted. It is probably instinctive for the infant to seek for the breast when placed near a large object; this occurs at a much younger age than the recognition of the bottle.

Scoring: Credit is given if the child indicates that he knows that food is coming when he sees the bottle. The usual successful response takes the form of increased activity, kicking, waving arms, vocalization, or opening the mouth.

3 Months

3. Regards Cube

Material: One one-inch wooden cube painted bright red.

Procedure: As the child is sitting in an upright position before the table the cube is placed on the table within easy view of the child. The cube may be tapped on the table or moved about to attract the child's attention.

Scoring: Credit is given if the child observes the cube. His eyes must remain on, or return to, the cube after the examiner has removed his hand. In other words the examiner must make sure that it is the cube and not his hand which is observed.

3 Months

4. Regards Spoon

Material: An aluminum teaspoon of standard size.

Procedure: The procedure and scoring is the same as for Regards Cube. As the child is sitting in an upright position before the table the spoon is placed within his easy view. The spoon may be tapped on the table or moved about to attract the child's attention.

Scoring: Credit is given if the child observes the spoon. His eyes must remain on, or return to, the spoon after the examiner has removed his hand.

3 Months

5. Inspects Fingers

Procedure: It must be determined whether or not the child has discovered his hands and inspects his fingers or fist as he moves them about. If the child does not demonstrate this ability while lying on the examining table, the mother can usually give a correct report on this point.

Scoring: Credit is given if the child observes his hands during the examination, or if he has been repeatedly observed to do so at home.

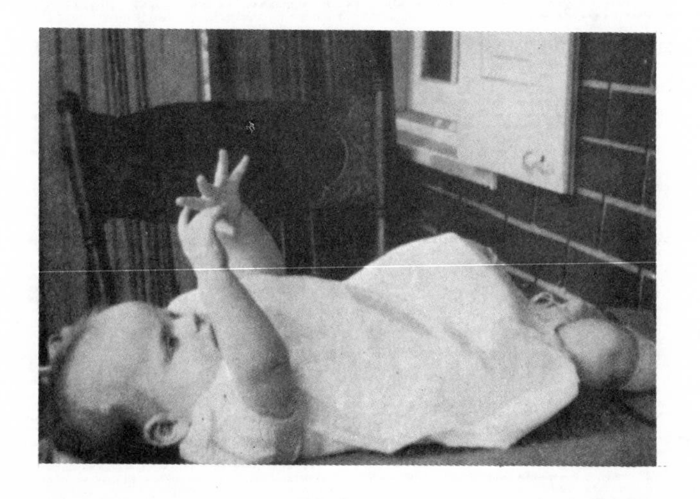

3 Months

Alternate a. LIFTS HEAD AND CHEST BY ARMS IN PRONE POSITION

Procedure: The child is placed face down on a soft but firm surface. The approximate height he is able to raise his chest at the suprasternal notch (space between the two shoulder blades) above the table is noted, and whether or not he uses his arms to support himself.

Scoring: Credit is given if the child raises his suprasternal notch at least two inches from the table and if he uses his arms to assist in holding his chest up. (Credit at two months if he raises his head.)

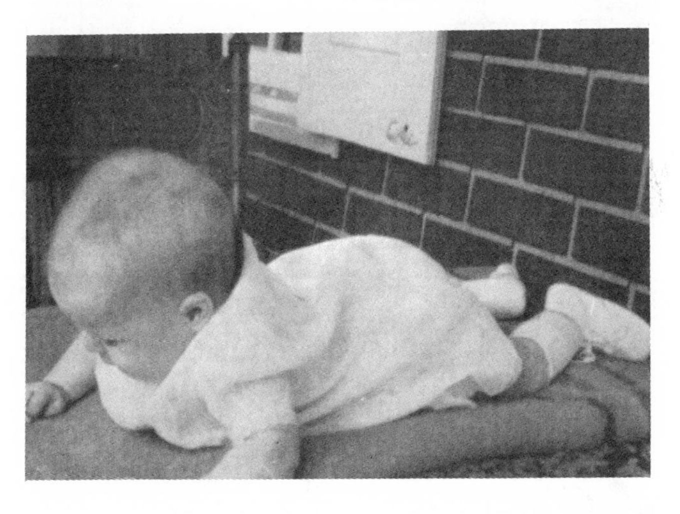

3 Months

Alternate b. HOLDS HEAD STEADY

Procedure: The child is placed in a sitting position on the edge of the table with the lower part of his legs hanging over the edge. He is supported by placing one hand over the ribs under each arm at the level of the nipples, care being taken not to hunch his shoulders.

Scoring: Credit is given if the child's head remains erect without wobbling while he is held in a stationary position.

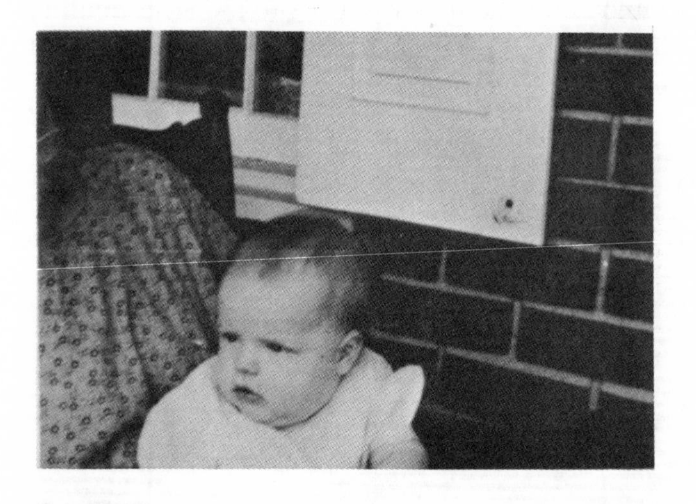

4 Months

1. Finger Manipulation

Procedure: It is determined either from observation or questioning whether or not the child in playing with his hands, fingers one hand with the other or grasps and regrasps his hands. An intelligent mother can usually give a correct report if what is meant by grasping and fingering is demonstrated.

Credit: Score plus if the child manipulates one hand with the other.

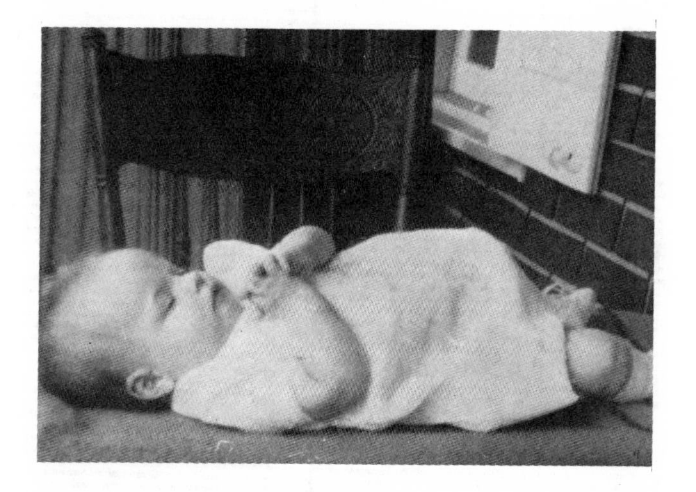

4 Months

2. Hands Remain Open

Procedure: The hands are observed during the examination to determine whether or not the fingers are curled and the fist closed as is characteristic of the new born infant or whether the hand is held in an open position. If the fist is closed, it is of interest to record whether the thumb is outside or enclosed within the fist.

Scoring: Credit is given if the hands remain open during at least one-half of the period of the examination.

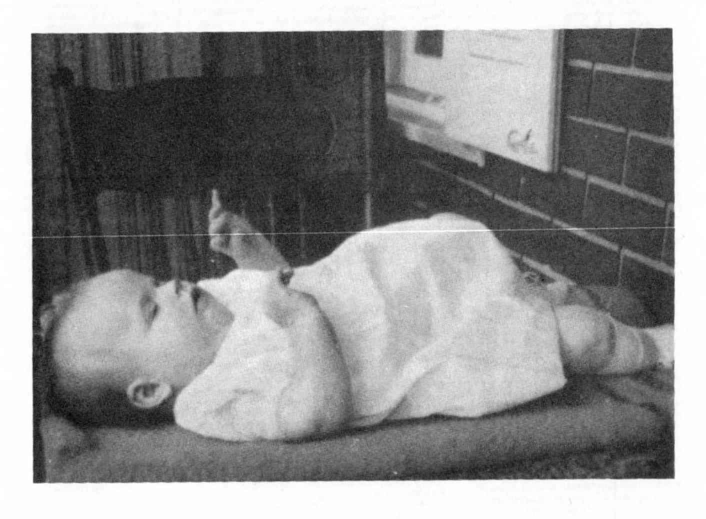

4 Months

3. Follows Ball across Table

Material: A bright red rubber ball one and one-half inches in diameter.

Procedure: The child should be seated before the table and the ball placed on the table to the right of the child, but within easy view, and his attention attracted to it. It is then rolled across the table in front of him to determine whether or not he can follow it with his eyes. If he fails to follow, or if the response is doubtful, the ball is rolled back and forth three or four times. The child's attention may be drawn to the ball by holding a cube in the palm of the hand and tapping it on the table just before starting the ball rolling.

Scoring: Credit is given if the child definitely follows the ball with his eyes.

4 Months

4. Turns to Voice

Procedure: As the child is sitting in an upright position on his mother's lap, the examiner, approaching the child from behind, brings his mouth directly in a line with the ears and about twelve inches distant. He then calls the child's name in a low, quiet voice. If there is no response, the procedure should be repeated several times—first on one side and then on the other.

Scoring: Credit is given if the child turns his head toward the voice. Care should be taken that he does not catch sight of the examiner and turn toward the visual rather than the auditory stimulus. Care must also be taken that the mother does not assist the child in turning.

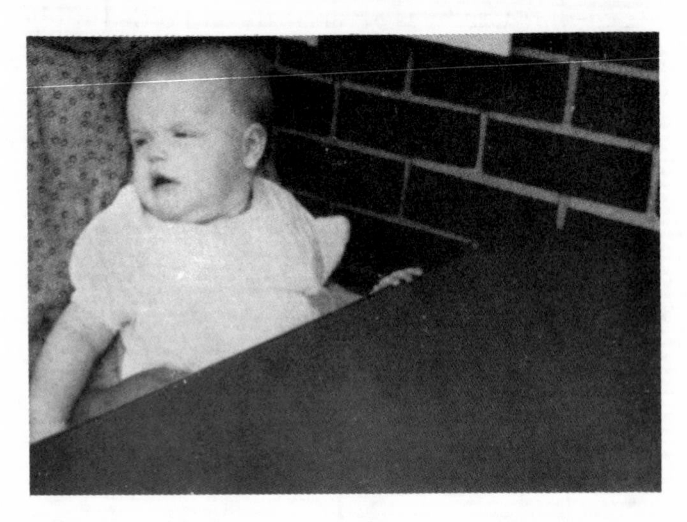

4 Months

5. Increases Activity at Sight of Toy

Material: Embroidery ring. (See page 99.)

Procedure: As the child is lying on his back, the ring is dangled by the string, about eight inches before his eyes, in the line of his vision. If the child is uninterested in the ring, a rattle may be used and gently shaken to attract his attention.

Scoring: Credit is given if there is a definite increase in the activity of the child when the ring or the rattle is presented. This usually takes the form of increased kicking and waving of the arms, often accompanied by facial movements.

4 Months

Alternate a. RECOVERS RATTLE FROM CHEST

Material: A small dumbbell-shaped rattle with balls about one and three-fourths inches in diameter and a stem three and one-half inches long.

Procedure: When the child is lying on his back the rattle is taken from him, shaken gently to attract his attention, then laid on his chest, this may be repeated several times. Next the rattle is placed on the table at the curve of the child's shoulder.

Scoring: Credit is given if the child makes an effort to secure the rattle and succeeds in either position. A chance success is not credited. If there is any doubt about the response it should be tried several times. (Credit is given at five months if he attains the rattle when placed at his shoulder.)

4 Months

Alternate b. PLAYS ACTIVELY WITH RATTLE

Material: Rattle. (See page 118.)

Procedure: The rattle is handed to the child as he is lying on his back, or, if necessary, placed within his hand, and his play with it observed.

Scoring: Credit is given if he actively waves, shakes, bangs or manipulates and observes the rattle. Credit is not given if he merely grasps and waves the rattle in a passive or reflex manner, or if the child reacts in the same manner as when his hands are empty.

5 Months

1. Turns to Bell

Material: A metal bell with wooden handle. The bell cup is about two inches in diameter and one and one-half inches deep. The handle is two and one-half inches long.

Procedure: The procedure is the same as for the voice. When the child is seated before the table, the bell is rung gently, directly in a line with the ears, and at a distance of about twelve inches. It is important that the bell be rung gently, as a loud ring may frighten the child. Several trials may be given on each side.

Scoring: Credit is given if the child turns toward the sound of the bell without the aid of visual stimulation.

5 Months

2. Attains Ring

Material: Embroidery ring. (See page 99.)

Procedure: As the child is lying on his back, the ring is dangled by the string in the line of his vision and about eight inches before his eyes.

Scoring: Credit is given if the child actually attains the ring within his grasp at least twice. It is not necessary that he should actually grasp the ring with one hand. The more common response at this age is to close in on it with both hands, sometimes with fists closed. (Credit is given for the second alternate item at this age if he pulls the ring toward him against resistance and at four months if he increases his activity or if he approaches the ring with his hands.)

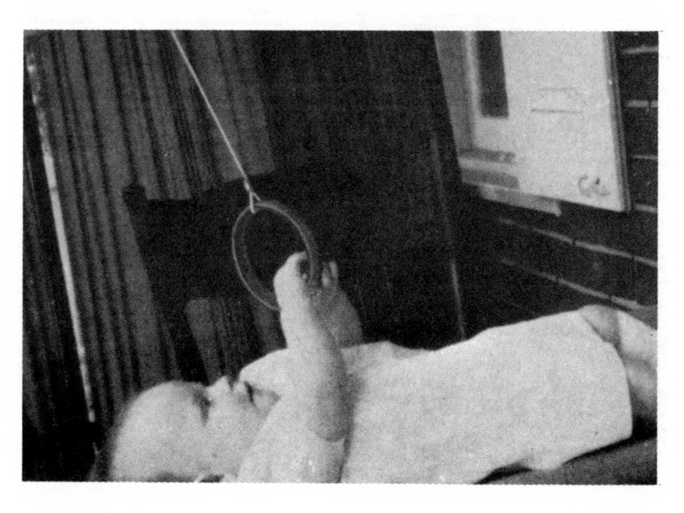

5 Months

3. Transfers Object from Hand to Hand

Material: Embroidery ring or rattle. (See pages 99 and 118.)

Procedure: The child, when lying on his back, is observed during his play with the rattle, the ring or other object in order to determine whether the child has learned to change an object from one hand to the other. The observations required for scoring this test may be made at the time some other item is being given in which the child has an opportunity to manipulate the ring or the rattle.

Scoring: Credit is given if either of the objects is changed from hand to hand two or more

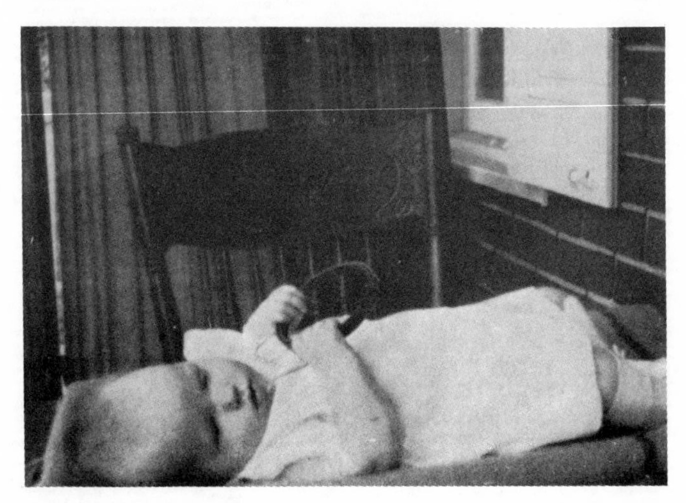

times. The child may also be given credit if the mother can give evidence that he habitually plays with objects in this manner at home. He should not be credited, however, if he has only been observed to do so when the free hand has come in contact with the object by chance.

5 Months

4. Regards Pellet

Material: Sugar pellet. The pellet is three-tenths of a millimeter in diameter, flat on one side and convex on the other. There is always danger of a child picking up a small object, putting it in his mouth and swallowing it before the examiner can intervene. It is, therefore, necessary that the pellet be harmless if swallowed.

Procedure: The pellet is placed on its convex surface on the table in front of the child (sitting position). The examiner may tap on the table, rock the pellet back and forth, or otherwise attract the child's attention to it. The child's reactions should be described, noting especially any of the following responses:

1. The child's eyes remain on, or return to the pellet after the examiner has removed his hand.
2. The child puts out his hands in an attempt to secure the pellet.
3. He succeeds in picking up the pellet. The earliest type of success is usually with a whole-hand raking movement.
4. The pellet is secured with a scissor-like movement of the thumb and finger, the palm of the hand remaining on or near the table. This

reaction is more mature than the raking whole-hand grasp.

5. A still higher form of response is an approach from above with a pincer-like motion of the thumb and index finger.

Scoring: Credit is given if the child merely observes the pellet, but care must be taken to insure that it is the pellet and not the examiner's hand that is being observed. (Credit is given at six months if there is an attempt to pick up the pellet.)

5 Months

5. Picks up Spoon

Material: Teaspoon. (See page 109.)

Procedure: The spoon is placed directly in front of the child (sitting position) within easy reach.

Scoring: Credit is given if the child makes a definite effort to reach for and pick up the spoon and succeeds, but if the spoon is picked up by reflex closure of the hand on chance contact it is not credited. Accurate reaching, however, is not to be expected at this age.

5 Months

Alternate a. Recovers Rattle from Shoulder

Material: Rattle. (See page 118.)

Procedure: The rattle is taken from the child and shaken gently to attract his attention, then it is laid on the table at his shoulder as he is lying on his back.

Scoring: Credit is given if the child makes an effort to secure the rattle and succeeds. (Credit is given at four months if he can pick the rattle up from his chest.)

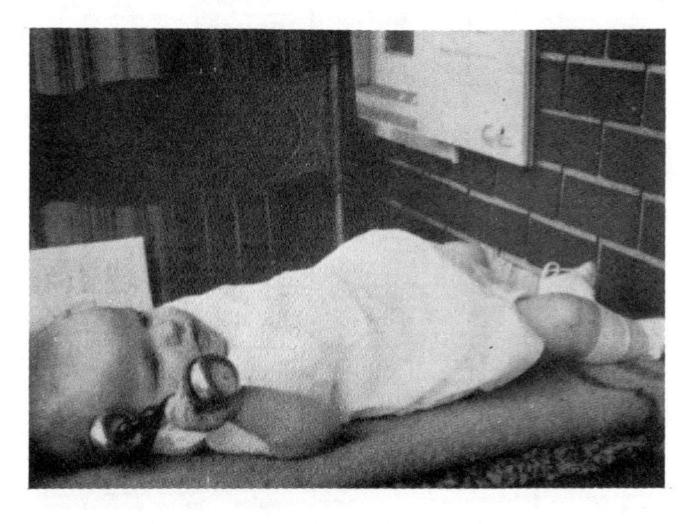

5 Months

Alternate b. Pulls Down Suspended Ring

Material: Embroidery ring. (See page 99.)

Procedure: While the child is lying on his back the ring is dangled above his head and he is encouraged to take hold of it, but the examiner keeps a firm hold on the string.

Scoring: Credit is given if the child pulls the ring toward him against the resistance of the examiner. (He also gets credit for Item 2 at this age if he attains the ring, without assistance, and at four months if he reaches for it.)

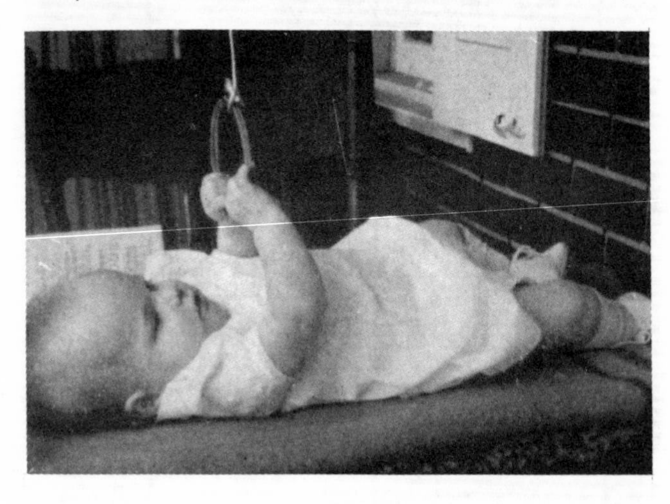

Test materials for ages six to eleven months inclusive.

6 Months

1. Secures Cube on Sight

Material: A one-inch cube. (See page 108.)

Procedure: When the child is sitting in an upright position before the table a cube is placed on the table within easy reach. The cube may be tapped on the table or moved about to attract the child's attention.

Scoring: Credit is given if the child is able to pick the cube up off the table. He is not credited if his hands should come in contact with the cube by chance and close on it reflexly.

6 Months

2. Lifts Cup

Material: The cup is aluminum with straight sides. Both the depth and the diameter of the rim are approximately three and one-half inches.

Procedure: The cup is placed upside down within easy reach of the child as he is sitting at the table.

Scoring: Credit is given if the child definitely picks up the cup and lifts it from the table.

6 Months

3. Fingers Reflection in Mirror

Material: A framed mirror fifteen by ten inches or larger. The mirror must be large enough to avoid the child's attention being distracted from his reflection by the desire to manipulate the mirror as a whole.

Procedure: While the child is in a sitting position, the mirror is held before him in such a manner that he can see his reflection, but not that of his mother or other persons.

Scoring: Credit is given if he reaches out and fingers his reflection. (He is given credit at seven months if he pats and smiles or talks to his reflection.)

6 Months

4. Reaches Unilaterally

Material: A door key or a peg between two and three inches in length.

Procedure: The child should sit with his shoulders square to the front and with both hands an equal distance from the examiner. The key is presented in the perpendicular position. This is repeated six times. If the child should lose interest in the key, a peg or other object of similar size may be used. Care must be taken that the shoulders are square to the front and the hands down before each presentation, also that the child does not reach with one hand merely because he has just done

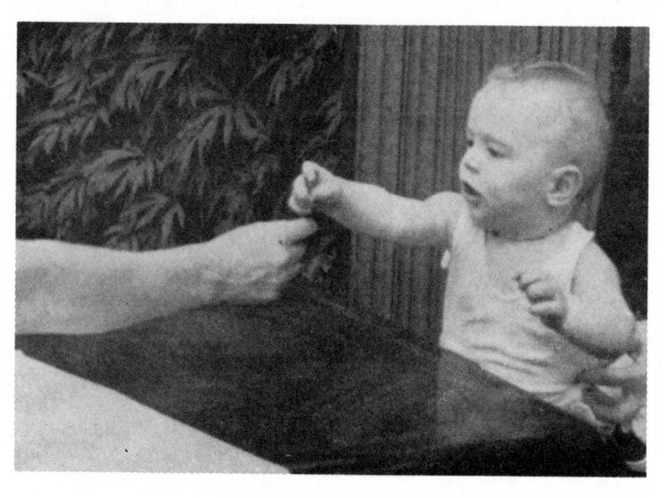

so and that hand is more ready to respond for that reason. It is well to allow him to manipulate the key or to give some other test item between trials.

Scoring: Credit is given if the child reaches for the objects with one hand in at least five of the six trials, or if when he reaches with both hands the one that grasps the object is at least three inches in advance of the other in five of the trials. (He is given credit at 8 months if he takes the object with the same hand in five of the six trials.)

6 Months

5. Reaches Persistently

Material: A cube (see page 108) or other object of approximately the same size.

Procedure: A cube is placed on the table just out of the child's reach. If the cube should not arouse the child's interest some other object of about the same size but of greater interest to the child may be used.

Scoring: Credit is given if the child either keeps his hand stretched toward the object for several seconds or, as more frequently happens, if he reaches toward the object several times.

6 Months

Alternate a. APPROACHES SECOND CUBE

Material: Four wooden one-inch cubes painted bright red.

Procedure: The child is first presented with one cube and as soon as he has taken it a second is held before him in such a position as to favor his grasping, but is not actually placed in his hand. If the second cube is taken a third is held up before him. Instead of attempting to hold two or three cubes some children will place them on the table before them. It is therefore better if the child sits on the edge of his mother's (or attendant's) knee in such a position that there

is no flat surface on which he can put the blocks within reach.

Scoring: Credit is given if the child approaches the second cube in an attempt to take hold of it, even if he is unable to attain the cube. (He is given credit at seven months if he takes hold of the second and at ten months if he attempts the third.)

7 Months

1. Attempts to Pick up Pellet

Material: Sugar pellet. (See page 124.)

Procedure: The pellet is placed on its convex surface on the table in front of the child. The table may be tapped or the pellet rocked back and forth, to attract the child's attention to it. The following responses should be recorded.

1. The child's eyes remain on, or return to the pellet after the examiner has removed his hand.
2. The child puts out his hands in an attempt to secure the pellet.
3. He succeeds in picking up the pellet. The earliest type of success is usually with a whole-hand raking movement.
4. The pellet is secured with a scissor-like movement of thumb and finger, the palm of the hand remaining on or near the table.
5. A still higher form of response is the pincer-like motion of thumb and finger from above.

Scoring: Credit is given if the child makes a definite effort to pick up the pellet, whether he is successful or not. (Credit is given at five months if he merely observes the pellet and at eight months if he succeeds in picking up the pellet.)

7 Months

2. Pats and Smiles at Reflection in Mirror

Material: Mirror. (See page 132.)

Procedure: While the child is sitting at the table, the mirror is held before him in such a position that he can readily see his own reflection, but not that of his mother or any other person.

Scoring: Credit is given if he pats and smiles, talks to or makes other playful responses toward his reflection. (He is given credit at six months if he reaches out to finger his reflection.)

7 Months

3. Inspects Ring

Material: Embroidery ring. (See page 99.)

Procedure: The ring is handed to the child and his behavior with it observed to note whether or not he examines it. This may be observed in connection with a previous item in which the child has had an opportunity to manipulate the ring.

Scoring: Credit is given if the child examines the ring with sustained attention as he manipulates it.

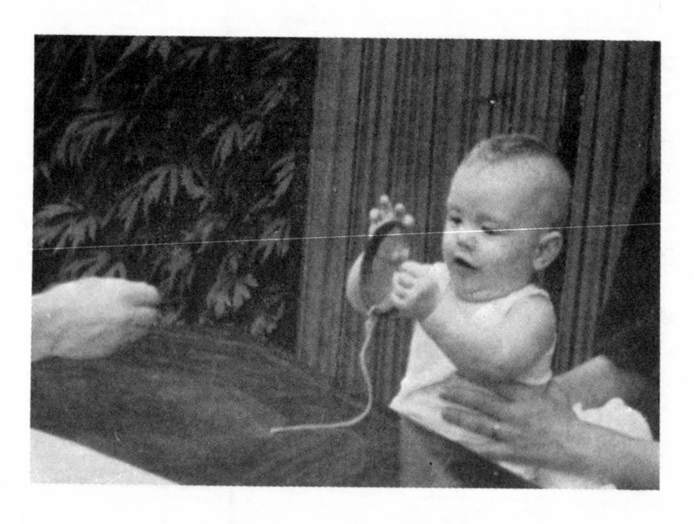

7 Months

4. Secures Two Cubes

Material: Four one-inch cubes. (See page 108.)

Procedure: The child is sitting away from the table, preferably on the edge of the mother's (or attendant's) knee, in such a position that there is no flat surface handy. He is first presented with one cube and as soon as he has taken it a second is held before him in such a position as to favor his grasping it, but it is not actually placed in his hand. If the second cube is taken a third is held up before him.

Scoring: Credit is given if the child takes the second cube and holds both for several seconds. (He is given credit at six months if he attempts to take the second and at ten months if there is an attempt to take the third cube.)

7 Months

5. Exploits Paper

Material: A sheet of onion-skin paper eight and one half by eleven inches.

Procedure: A piece of onion-skin paper is presented to the child, edge first.

Scoring: Credit is given if the child actively waves, exploits or otherwise plays with the paper in a purposeful manner.

7 Months

Alternate a. Grasps String

Material: A round shoestring fifteen inches long and of a color that contrasts with the table top.

Procedure: The shoestring is placed on the table before the child and his attention attracted to it by pointing, tapping on the table, etc.

Scoring: Credit is given if the child is able to pick up the string.

7 Months

Alternate b. Pulls out Peg

Material: The Wallin Peg Board A. The board is fourteen inches long, three inches wide and three-fourths of an inch thick, with a row of six holes down the center. The holes are placed two inches apart. In Peg Board A the holes are round and six-sixteenths of an inch in diameter. The pegs are two and one-half inches long and are just small enough to fit in the holes without binding.

Procedure: The Wallin Peg Board A is placed before the child, then a peg is placed in one of the holes within easy reach of the child. It is pulled out and reinserted several times and then left in place before the child. The child is encouraged by word and gesture to do the same.

Scoring: Credit is given if the child succeeds in removing the peg two or more times.

8 Months

1. Attains Ring by Pulling String

Material: Embroidery ring. (See page 99.)

Procedure: The ring is placed on the table outside the child's reach with the string toward him and within easy reach. If the child lacks interest in the ring, the bell or some other object of interest may be placed within the ring.

Scoring: Credit is given if the child pulls the ring toward him by means of the string at least twice. If on the first trial he pulls the string with an obviously purposeful movement there is no need to give a second trial.

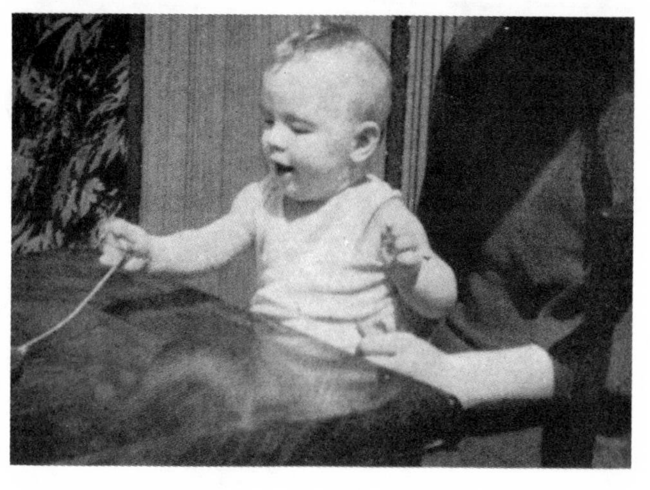

8 Months

2. Manipulates String

Material: A shoestring. (See page 143.)

Procedure: The shoestring is placed on the table before the child.

Scoring: Credit is given if the child is interested in manipulating and examining the string.

8 Months

3. Combines Two Syllables in Vocal Play

Procedure: It is determined, through questioning the mother, or otherwise, whether or not the child in his vocal play utters such syllables as "da-da," "ma-ma," "ba-ba," etc.

Scoring: Credit is given if any double syllables such as the above are spoken during vocal play. A few children, when crying make sounds that sound like "ma-ma." This is not credited, but if "ma-ma" is uttered in vocal play credit is given.

8 Months

4. Secures Pellet

Material: Sugar pellet. (See page 124.)

Procedure: The pellet is placed on its convex surface on the table in front of the child. The table may be tapped or the pellet rocked back and forth to attract the child's attention to it. The child's reactions should be described, noting especially any of the following responses:

1. The child's eyes remain on, or return to, the pellet after the examiner has removed his hand.
2. The child puts out his hands in an attempt to secure the pellet.
3. He succeeds in picking up the pellet with a raking movement of the fingers.

4. The pellet is secured with scissor-like movement between the thumb and finger, the palm of the hand remaining on or near the table.

5. A still higher form of response is the pincer-like movement of the thumb and finger from above.

Scoring: Credit is given if the child succeeds in picking up the pellet by any method. The earliest form of success is usually with a whole-hand raking movement. (He is given credit at six months if he makes an attempt to pick up the pellet and at nine if he picks it up with the scissor-like grasp.)

8 Months

5. Inspects Details of Bell

Material: A bell. (See page 120.)

Procedure: The bell is placed on the table with the cup toward the child and his manipulations observed. Care must be taken not to ring the bell as it is presented. Should the child accidently learn how to ring it and become so interested in ringing that he has no desire to examine the bell the item must be scored as omitted and an alternate given in its place.

Scoring: Credit is given if the child shows interest in examining the clapper in the inside of the bell cup.

8 Months

Alternate a. Hand Preference

Material: A key or a peg. (See page 133.)

Procedure: For this item the child should be sitting with his shoulders square to the front and with both hands an equal distance from the examiner. The key is presented to him in the perpendicular position directly in front of him. This is repeated six times. If the child should lose interest in the key, a peg or the spoon may be used. Care must be taken that the shoulders are square to the front and the hands down before each presentation, also that the child does not reach with one hand merely because he has just done so and that hand is more ready to respond for that reason. It is well to allow him to manipulate the key for a few moments or to give some other test between trials.

Scoring: Credit is given if the child reaches for and grasps the object with the same hand in five out of six trials. (Credit is given at six months if he reaches with one hand rather than both in five of the six trials.)

8 Months

Alternate b. Bangs Spoon

Material: A teaspoon. (See page 109.)

Procedure: The spoon is knocked on the table in front of the child and then presented to him. While he is playing with the spoon, it is taken from him and again knocked against the table (care must be taken not to startle him) and returned to him. If the child does not imitate, the demonstration should be repeated several times.

Scoring: Credit is given if the child bangs the spoon against the table, or if his mother or attendant can give evidence that he does so frequently at home.

9 Months

1. SECURES PELLET WITH SCISSOR-LIKE GRASP

Material: Sugar pellet. (See page 124.)

Procedure: The pellet is placed on its convex surface on the table in front of the child. The table may be tapped or the pellet rocked back and forth to attract the child's attention to it. The child's reactions should be described, noting especially any of the following responses:

1. The child puts out his hands in an attempt to secure the pellet.
2. He succeeds in picking up the pellet. The earliest type of success is usually with a whole-hand raking movement.
3. The pellet is secured with a scissor-like movement from the side of the thumb and finger, the palm of the hand remaining on or near the table. This reaction is more mature than the raking whole-hand grasp.
4. A still higher form of response is the pincer-like motion of the thumb and finger from above.

Scoring: Credit is given if the pellet is picked up between the thumb and index or middle finger. (Credit is given at eight if he picks up the pellet by any method and at eleven months if he picks it up with an over-head, pincer-like grasp.)

9 Months

2. Looks for Spoon

Material: A teaspoon. (See page 109.)

Procedure: The table is moved so that the child is sitting near the corner. The spoon is knocked on the edge of the table and the child's attention attracted to it, then it is dropped out of sight. Care must be taken that there is no noise as of dropping on the floor when the spoon disappears. The purpose of the test is to determine whether or not the child attempts to follow a disappearing visual stimulus, not his response to an auditory stimulus.

Scoring: Credit is given if the child turns to look for the spoon.

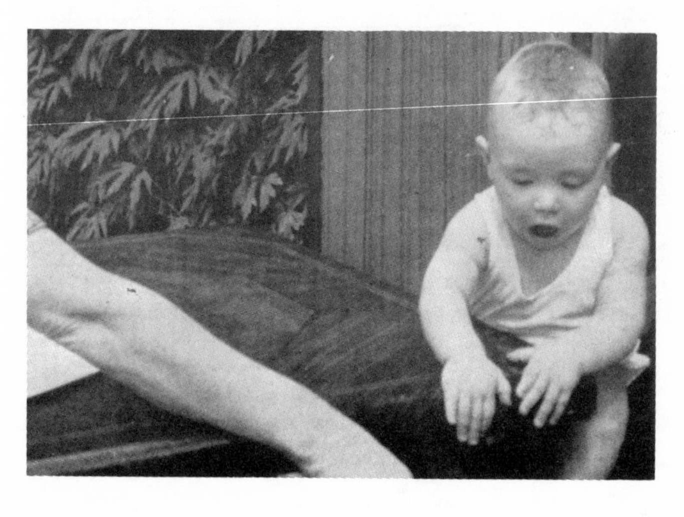

9 Months

3. Rings Bell

Material: A dinner bell. (See page 120.)

Procedure: The bell is rung gently, while it is being presented to the child, or it is taken from him after he has been given it to inspect, gently rung and returned to him with the words, "—— (child's name) do." Care must be taken to ring the bell gently in order not to startle the child.

Scoring: Credit is given if the child rings the bell in imitation of the examiner.

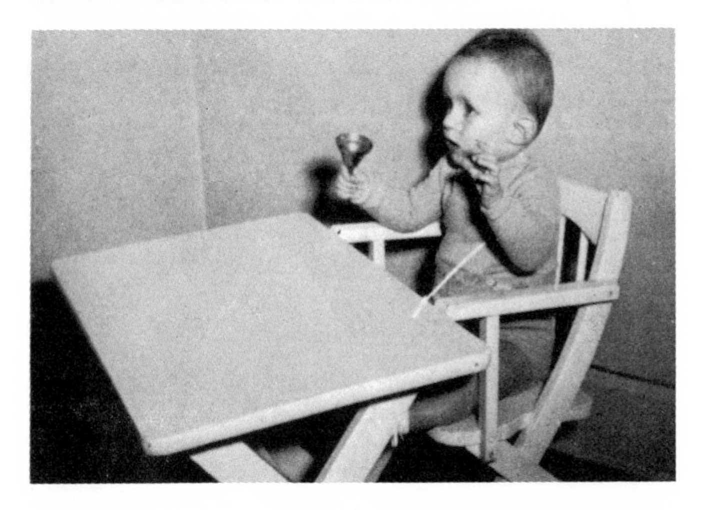

9 Months

4. Adjusts to Gesture

Procedure: It is determined whether or not the child has learned any tricks that he will perform on request by word or gesture from the mother or other persons, such as "pat-a-cake," wave hand for "bye-bye," hands up for "how big is the baby," etc. It will usually be necessary to depend on the mother's report, which should be recorded in full.

Scoring: Credit is given if the child has any such "trick" which he is willing to demonstrate (if in a favorable mood), when requested by word or gesture.

9 Months

5. Adjusts to Words

Procedure: It must be determined whether or not the child has learned to perform any act in response to a spoken request. (It will usually be necessary to depend on the mother's report.) The earliest responses are most frequently waves in response to "bye-bye," claps hands in response to "pat-a-cake," looks toward the object in response to "Where is kitty?" "Where is the light?" "Where is the clock?" "Where is daddy?" etc.

Scoring: Credit is given if the child, when in a favorable mood, responds in an appropriate manner to any verbal request unaccompanied by a gesture.

9 Months

Alternate a. Imitates Sounds

Procedure: Through questioning the mother, it is determined whether or not the child imitates any sounds that she makes such as coughing, grunting, smacking lips, etc.

Scoring: Credit is given if it can be determined that the child imitates a sound.

10 Months

1. Uncovers Toy

Material: A small opaque handkerchief or a piece of cloth approximately ten by ten inches and a small twelve-inch string of brightly colored beads about three-sixteenths of an inch in diameter, or some other small toy attractive to the child.

Procedure: The small string of beads, or other object, is placed on the table before the child and covered with the handkerchief while he is watching.

Scoring: Credit is given if the child removes the handkerchief with the purpose of securing the object. He is not credited if he removes the handkerchief by accident, nor is credit given if in picking it up or pushing it aside his interest centers on the handkerchief rather than the hidden object.

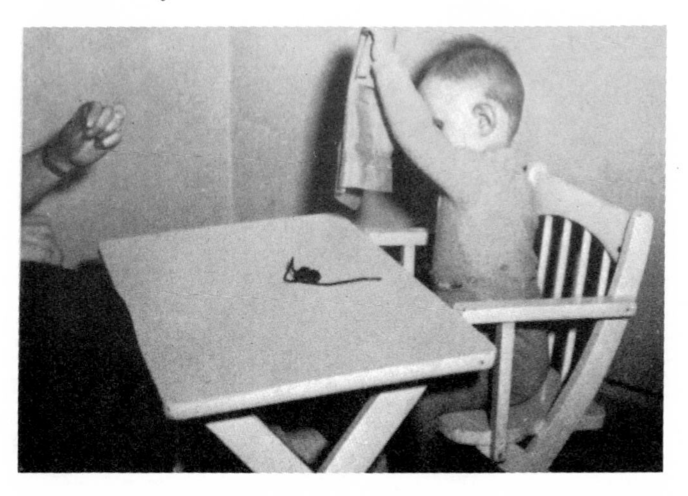

10 Months

2. Combines Cup and Cube

Material: An aluminum cup and a one-inch cube. (See pages 108 and 131.)

Procedure: The cup and cube are placed before the child and his behavior observed. This may be done in connection with the item "Secures Toy from under Cup."

Scoring: Credit is given if the child in his manipulation of the cup and cube plays with them in combination, such as hitting the cup with the cube, putting the cube in the cup, etc. If the child's attention is drawn first to one object, then the other, and he apparently forgets one while he examines or manipulates the other, no credit is given.

10 Months

3. Attempts to Take Third Cube

Material: Four one-inch cubes. (See page 108).

Procedure: Preferably the child should sit away from the table, on the edge of the mother's (or attendant's) knee, in such a position that there is no flat surface handy. When sitting at a table some children will place the cubes on the table before them instead of making any attempt to hold all three or even two. He is first presented with one cube and as soon as he has taken it, a second is held before him in such a position as to favor his grasping it, but it is not actually

placed in his hand. If the second cube is taken, a third is held up before him.

Scoring: Credit is given if the child drops one of the two cubes he has in his hands and takes the offered third one, or if he puts out one or both hands with a cube in them and tries, even though unsuccessfully, to take the third. (Credit is given at seven months for taking two cubes and at 14 for taking three.)

10 Months

4. Hits Cup with Spoon

Material: Aluminum cup and teaspoon. (See pages 109 and 131.)

Procedure: The cup is placed before the child and the spoon moved back and forth in it, hitting the edges. The spoon is then placed beside the cup with handle toward the child.

Scoring: Credit is given if the child hits the cup with the spoon two or three times either inside or outside. (Credit is given at twelve months if the spoon is placed within the cup and is moved back and forth.)

10 Months

5. Pokes Fingers in Holes of Peg Board

Material: Wallin Peg Board A. (See page 144.)

Procedure: The board is placed before the child and the holes pointed out by poking the forefinger into first one and then another saying, "See."

Scoring: Credit is given if the child pokes his fingers into one of the holes.

10 Months

Alternate a. PICKS UP SPOON BEFORE CUP

Material: A cup and a teaspoon. (See pages 109 and 131.)

Procedure: The spoon and the cup are placed side by side on the table before the child and his behavior observed. The spoon should be placed directly in front of the child and about two inches to right of the cup. If the cup is picked up first, repeat twice, first placing the cup to the right of the spoon then to the left.

Scoring: Credit is given if the spoon is picked up before the cup in the first trial or in two of three trials.

11 Months

1. SECURES PELLET WITH A PINCER-LIKE GRASP

Material: Sugar pellet. (See page 124.)

Procedure: The pellet is placed on its convex surface on the table in front of the child. The table may be tapped or the pellet rocked back and forth to attract the child's attention to it. The child's reactions should be described, noting especially any of the following responses:

1. The child succeeds in picking up the pellet. The earliest type of success is usually with a whole-hand raking movement.

2. The pellet is secured with scissor-like movement of the thumb and finger, the palm of

the hand remaining on or near the table. This reaction is more mature than the raking whole-hand grasp.

3. A still higher form of response is the pincer-like motion of the thumb and finger from above.

Scoring: Credit is given if the child picks up the pellet with an over-hand pincer-like movement of the thumb and index or middle finger. (Credit is given at eight months if the pellet is picked up with the scissor-like movement of thumb and finger.)

11 Months

2. Secures Toy from under Cup

Material: Cup and string of beads or other small toy. (See pages 131 and 159.)

Procedure: The string of beads, or other object of interest to the child, is placed on the table before him and as he is about to pick it up the cup is placed over it with the handle to his right. Two or three trials may be given. The handle is placed to the left of the child in the second trial.

Scoring: Credit is given if in one of the three trials the child lifts the cup and immediately secures the toy. Credit is not given if he picks up the toy only after his eyes have fallen on it by chance.

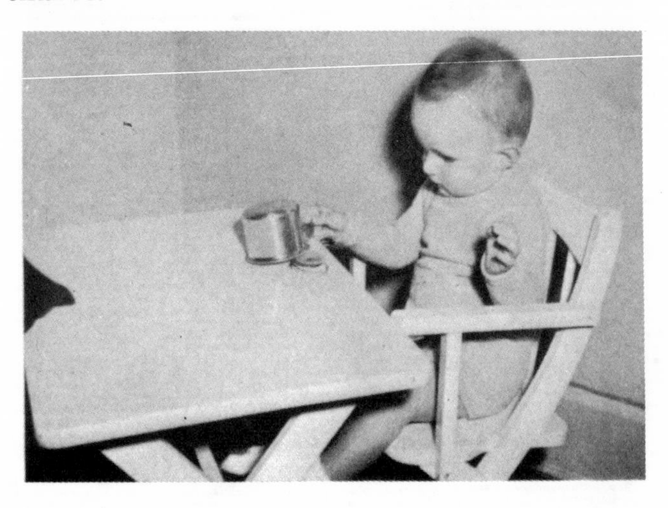

11 Months

3. Looks for Contents of Box

Material: A box, with ends approximately one and one-half inches square and about three inches high, open at one end and two stones about three-fourths inch in diameter. Dice or other objects of the same size may be used in place of the stones.

Procedure: The two stones or other small objects should be placed in the box and gently rattled then emptied on the table before the child and almost immediately returned to the box and again gently shaken. It is important that the child watch the whole procedure. Finally the box is momentarily held out of the

child's field of vision, the stones removed and then the empty box given to him. If the child does not almost immediately give evidence that he is looking for the stones the procedure is repeated with the exception that this time the box is handed to him with the stones still inside.

Scoring: Credit is given if the child looks disappointed when he looks in the box on the first trial or gives other evidence that he expected to find the stones or if he clearly shows that he is looking for the stones in the second trial.

11 Months

4. Speaking Vocabulary—One Word

Procedure: The mother's report must usually be depended upon in determining the number of words spoken by the child. It often helps in evaluating her report to ask when the word is used and how it sounds. "Ma-ma" and "da-da" are not credited as words as it is very difficult to determine whether they are spoken in vocal play or whether they are associated with the mother and father. The mother usually thinks that she is being called as soon as the child utters the syllables "ma-ma," while actually he usually uses them in vocal play several weeks or even months before he associates any meaning with them.

Scoring: Credit is given if the child has any word or syllable other than "da-da" or "ma-ma" which he uses to designate some definite object or situation.

11 Months

5. Places Cube in or over Cup

Material: A cup and a cube. (See pages 131 and 108.)

Procedure: The cup and the cube are placed before the child on the table and he is asked to put the "block" in the cup, as the examiner points first to the cube and then to the cup. If there is no response the examiner places the cube in the cup and then puts it again beside the cup saying, "——— do." If the child is successful, nine more cubes are pushed toward him with the words, "put them all in." No other help is given.

Scoring: Credit is given if the child places a cube in or over the cup. It is not necessary that he should release the cube. (If he puts a cube in the cup and releases it from his grasp he is given credit at twelve months.)

11 Months

Alternate a. Squeezes Doll

Material: A six-inch jointless rubber doll with a whistle. It should be made of soft rubber so that a light touch will cause a squeak.

Procedure: The jointless rubber doll is placed face up on the table before the child. It is hit gently several times with the open hand. Care must be taken not to cause more than a gentle squeak in the demonstration as there is danger of frightening the child by a loud one. If the child makes no attempt to hit the doll after two or three trials, the doll is picked up and squeezed gently several times and then handed to the child. This may be repeated two or three times.

Scoring: Credit is given if the child either hits or squeezes the doll. (Credit is given at twelve months if the child hits the doll in imitation of the examiner.)

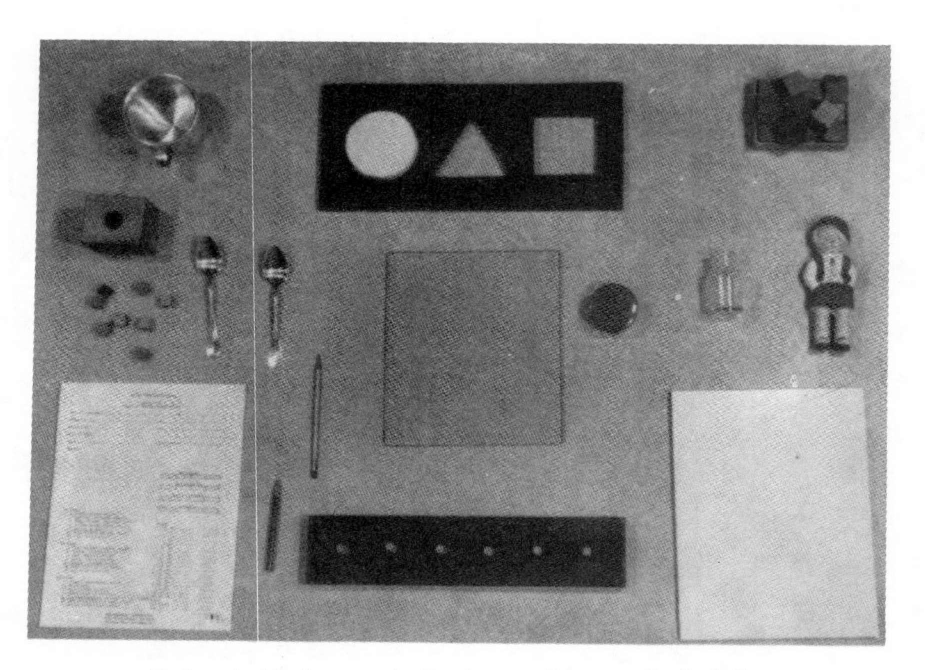

Test materials for ages twelve to seventeen months inclusive.

12 Months

1. Beats Two Spoons Together

Material: Two teaspoons. (See page 109.)

Procedure: One spoon is taken in each hand and they are beaten together gently while the child is watching, then they are presented to the child, one in each hand. If the child does not hit the spoons together in imitation of the examiner, the demonstration is repeated.

Scoring: Credit is given if the child hits one spoon with the other at least three times.

12 Months

2. Places One Cube in Cup

Material: Ten one-inch wooden cubes, painted bright red, and an aluminum cup with straight sides and with both the depth and the diameter of the rim approximately three and one-half inches.

Procedure: The cup and a cube are placed before the child on the table and he is asked to put the "block" in the cup, pointing first to the cube and then to the cup. If there is no response, the cube is put in the cup, then taken out and placed beside the cup with the request "——— (child's name) do." The demonstration may be repeated two or three times. If the child is suc-

cessful, nine more cubes are pushed toward him with the words, "Put them all in." No other instructions or help should be given.

Scoring: Credit is given if the child puts a cube in the cup and releases it from his grasp. (Credit is given at eleven months if one cube is placed in the cup even though the child does not release his grasp on the cube and at eighteen months if all ten are placed in the cup.)

12 Months

3. Marks with Pencil

Material: Pencil and paper. The pencil should not be longer than three and one-half inches nor shorter than two and one-half inches. The lead should be soft and the point blunt. Red or blue lead is preferable to black. An unused page of the examination blank may be used for the child to write on, or a blank sheet of paper of similar size and weight.

Procedure: A piece of paper and a pencil are placed before the child with the request "——— write." If after five or ten seconds he does not scribble. The paper and pencil are taken from him and again placed before him with the same

request. If there is still no response, the examiner takes the pencil and demonstrates by scribbling six to eight lines back and forth, about three inches in length, and then places the pencil on the table before the child again. This may be repeated if need be.

Scoring: Credit is given if the child makes any kind of marks on the paper. (If he makes a definite scribble, he is given credit at fourteen months and if he does so without demonstration, he is credited at eighteen months.)

12 Months

4. Rattles Spoon in Cup

Material: Cup and teaspoon. (See pages 131 and 109.)

Procedure: The cup is placed before the child and the spoon moved back and forth in it, hitting the edges; then the spoon is placed beside the cup with the handle toward the child. Repeat demonstration if need be, placing the spoon on the other side of the cup.

Scoring: Credit is given if the child puts the spoon in the cup and moves it back and forth, hitting the edges in imitation of the examiner. (He is given credit at ten months if he only hits the outside of the cup.)

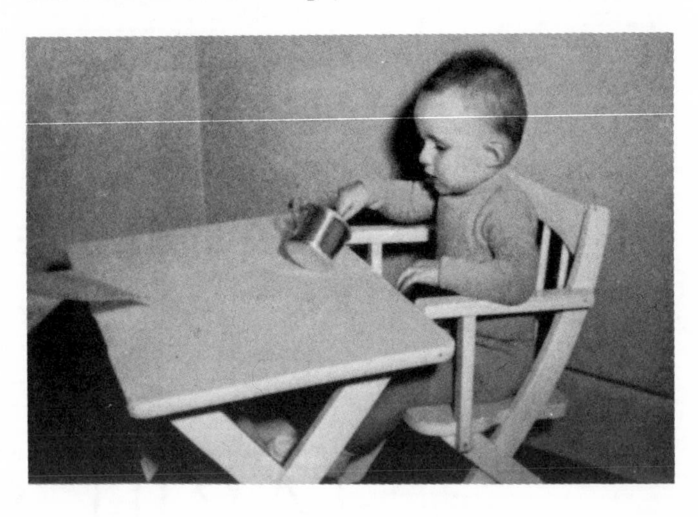

12 Months

5. Speaking Vocabulary—Two Words

Procedure: The mother's report must usually be depended upon in determining the number of words spoken by the child. It often helps in evaluating her report to ask when the word is used and how it sounds. "Ma-ma" and "da-da" are not credited as words as it is very difficult to determine whether they are spoken in vocal play or whether they are associated with the mother and the father. The mother usually thinks that she is being called as soon as the child utters the syllables "ma-ma," while in most instances he uses them in vocal play several weeks or even months before he associates any meaning with them.

Scoring: Credit is given if the child has a speaking vocabulary of two or more words. Any word or syllable other than "da-da" or "ma-ma" which the child uses to designate some definite object or situation is credited as a word. The "word" must not be applied indiscriminately to a number of stimuli. (Credit is given at eleven months for one word and at fourteen months for three words.)

12 Months

Alternate a. Hits Doll

Material: Jointless rubber doll with a whistle. (See page 173.)

Procedure: The rubber doll is placed face up on the table before the child. It is hit gently with an open hand several times. Care must be taken not to cause more than a gentle squeak in the demonstration as there is danger of frightening the child by a loud noise. If the child makes no attempt to hit the doll after two or three trials, it is picked up and squeezed gently two or three times and then handed to him. If he does not squeeze the doll, the procedure is repeated once or twice.

Scoring: Credit is given if the child makes a definite attempt to hit the doll even if he can not hit hard enough to produce a squeak. (Credit is given at eleven months if he produces a squeak by squeezing the doll.)

14 Months

1. Speaking Vocabulary—Three Words

Procedure: The mother's report must usually be depended upon in determining the number of words spoken by the child. It often helps in evaluating her report to ask when the word is used and how it sounds. "Ma-ma" and "da-da" are not credited as words, as it is very difficult to determine whether they are spoken in vocal play or whether they are associated with the mother and the father. The mother usually thinks that she is being called as soon as the child utters the syllables "ma-ma," while actually he usually uses them in vocal play several weeks or even months before he associates any meaning with them.

Scoring: Credit is given if the child has a speaking vocabulary of three or more words. Any word or syllable other than "da-da" or "ma-ma" which the child uses to designate some definite object or situation is credited as a word. The "word" must not be applied indiscriminately to a number of stimuli.

14 Months

2. Unwraps Toy

Material: Cube (see page 108) and a sheet of onion skin paper eight and one-half by eleven inches.

Procedure: While the child is watching, a cube, or some other object in which he is interested, is wrapped in a loose bag-like bundle with a sheet of onion skin paper. The child is asked to "get the block."

Scoring: Credit is given if the child secures the block in a purposeful manner. Do not credit if the block falls out accidentally as the child manipulates the paper without looking for the cube.

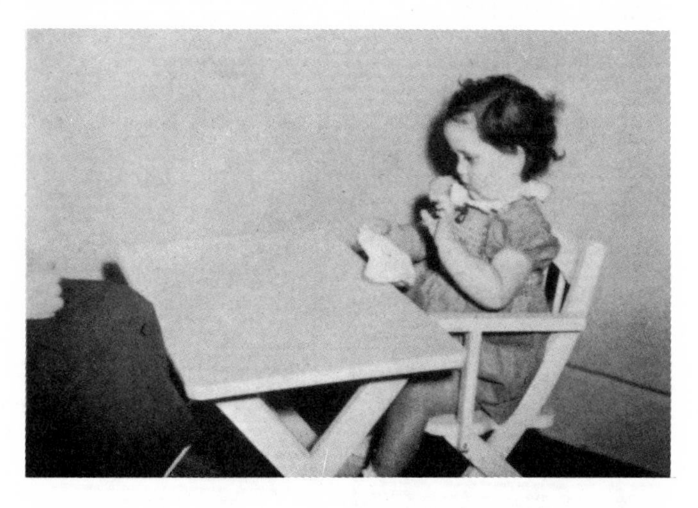

14 Months

3. Reaches Around Glass for Toy

Material: A piece of plate glass nine by eight inches, with ground edges, and a small toy.

Procedure: The piece of plate glass is held on its short edge in front of the child and a small toy that is attractive to him such as a string of beads, cat or doll, etc., is placed behind it. The glass must be held firmly as some children attempt to push it away with a surprising amount of strength. If possible, it should be placed against the rim of the table (see page 72), and held firmly with one hand at each of the upper corners.

Scoring: Credit is given if the child reaches around the glass and secures the toy.

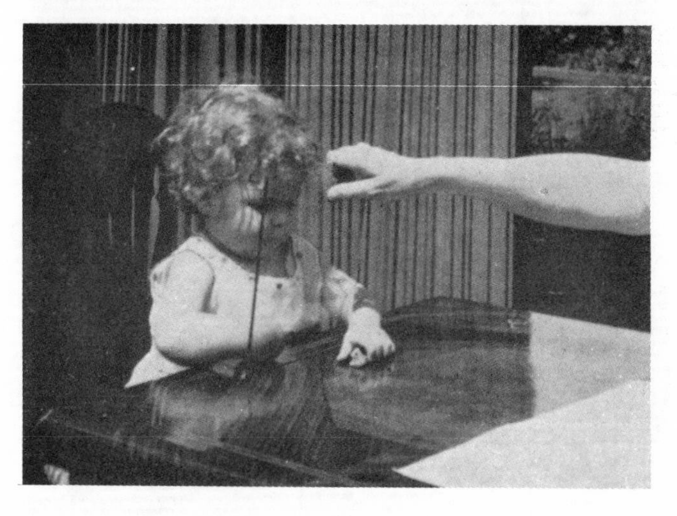

14 Months

4. Imitates Removal of Pellet from Bottle

Material: Sugar pellet (see page 124) and bottle. The bottle is the type with a glass stopper that is commonly used by biologists for preserving specimens. The height is three inches, the inside of the mouth 15/16 of an inch and the outside of the bottle one and one-half inches.

Procedure: The pellet and bottle are placed simultaneously side by side before the child. If the child does not spontaneously put the pellet in the bottle, he is asked to do so, or it is taken from him and dropped in the bottle, with the request: "Now get it out." If the child is unable

to discover for himself how to get the pellet from the bottle, it is emptied out and put back several times while he is watching. Then the bottle is placed before him with the pellet in it, with the words, "Now ——— get it." Additional trials should be given if there is doubt as to whether the pellet was removed by chance or by a purposeful act.

Scoring: Credit is given if the child removes the pellet from the bottle in a purposeful manner either before or after demonstration. Credit is not given if the pellet drops accidentally from the bottle during the child's manipulation. (Credit is given at sixteen months if he solves the problem without demonstration.)

14 Months

5. Pulls out and Replaces Peg in Peg Board A

Material: Wallin Peg Board A. (See page 144.)

Procedure: Peg Board A is placed before the child with one peg standing. While he is watching the peg is pulled out and replaced several times, then the board is pushed toward him and he is encouraged to pull out and replace the peg.

Scoring: Credit is given if the child places the peg at least twice. (He receives credit at seven months if he is able to remove pegs from the board and at eighteen months if he puts them all in.)

14 Months

Alternate a. Secures Third Cube

Material: Three one-inch wooden cubes painted bright red.

Procedure: The child is first presented with one cube and, as soon as he has taken it, a second is held before him in such a position as to favor his grasping, but is not actually placed in his hand. If the second cube is taken, a third is held up before him. Instead of attempting to hold all three cubes some children will place them on the table before them. It is therefore better if the child sits on the edge of the mother's (or attendant's) knee, in such a position that there is no flat surface within reach.

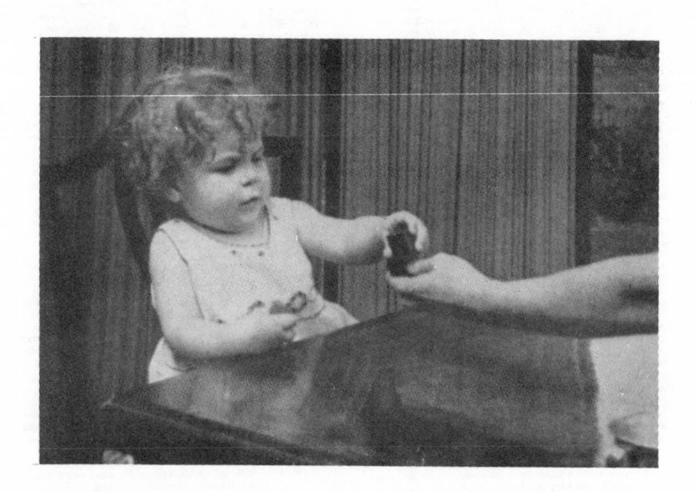

Scoring: Credit is given if the child is able to take and hold three cubes at one time by any method. Two cubes may be taken in one hand or the third cube may be held against the body, between the two closed fists or in the mouth. (Credit is given at ten months if he attempts to take the third cube.)

14 Months

Alternate b. Uncovers Box

Material: A round box and cat or other small toy. The round box is two inches in diameter and one inch in depth. The cover must not extend the whole way down the side of the box and the material must be sufficiently resistant to pressure so that it will not be forced out of shape during a child's clumsy attempts to fit on the cover.

Procedure: As the child is watching, the cat or other small toy is placed in the box and the box closed. The box is then opened and the toy removed, after which it is replaced in the box and the cover put back. The closed box is then

handed to him with the request, "——— get the kitty." The demonstration may be repeated two or three times and if there is need to increase the child's interest different objects may be enclosed within the box.

Scoring: Credit is given if the child is able to remove the cover at least twice. (Credit is given at sixteen months for closing the round box and at twenty-two months for closing an oblong one.)

16 Months

1. Places Round Block in Formboard

Material: The formboard is similar to Gesell's. It is made of a three-eighth inch board 36 × 16 cm., stained dark green. Three holes are cut in the board equidistant from each other and from the edges. From left to right the holes are a circle 8.7 cm. in diameter; an equilateral triangle, with sides 9.3 cm., and a square with sides 7.5 cm. The inserts are made of wood 2 cm. thick and painted white. The circle is 8.5 cm. in diameter, the sides of the triangle 9 cm., and those of the square 7.3 cm.

Procedure: The formboard is placed before the child with the circle on his left and the base

of the triangle toward him. The circle is placed in its recess and the child is allowed to take it out, then he is asked with appropriate gestures to, "Now put it back."

Scoring: Credit is given if the child replaces the round block. If it is done with an evidently purposeful act, one trial is enough, but if there is some doubt as to whether or not it was a chance replacement, no credit should be given unless it is placed a second time. (Credit is given for replacing the round block in the reversed board at eighteen months.)

16 Months

2. Speaking Vocabulary—Five Words

Procedure: The mother's report must usually be depended upon in determining the number of words spoken by the child. It often helps in evaluating her report to ask when the word is used and how it sounds. "Ma-ma" and "da-da" are not credited as words because it is very difficult to determine whether they are spoken in vocal play or whether they are associated with the mother and the father. The mother usually thinks that she is being called as soon as the child utters the syllables "ma-ma," while actually he usually uses them in vocal play several weeks or even months before he associates any meaning with them. Any word or syllable other than "da-da" or "ma-ma" which the child uses to designate some definite object or situation is credited as a word. The "word" must not be applied indiscriminately to a number of stimuli.

Scoring: Credit is given if the child has a speaking vocabulary of five words or more. (Credit is given for three words at fourteen months.)

16 Months

3. Puts Beads in Box

Material: Eight square kindergarten beads one-half inch square and a covered box with top and bottom two inches square and a height of three and one-half inches. There is a round hole one inch in diameter through the center of the cover.

Procedure: The eight square beads are emptied from the box onto the table in front of the child and the closed box with the hole uppermost placed beside them. The examiner picks up a bead and holds it momentarily over the hole before dropping it into the box, saying as he does so, "See they go in here. ——— put

some in" (using the child's name) "put them all in." If the child does not then start putting the beads in the examiner encourages him by repeating the verbal instructions and pointing first to the beads and then to the hole. If he still does not respond correctly another bead may be placed by the examiner as above with the words "See, now ——— do, put them all in." No further help is given.

Scoring: Credit is given if the remaining six beads are picked up and dropped in the hole without further urging.

16 Months

4. Solves Pellet and Bottle Problem

Material: Sugar pellet and bottle. (See pages 124 and 187.)

Procedure: The pellet and bottle are placed simultaneously before the child side by side. If the child does not spontaneously put the pellet in the bottle, he is asked to do so, or it is taken from him and dropped into the bottle, saying, "Now get it out." Should there be any doubt as to whether the child has removed the pellet by chance or by purposeful activity additional trials should be given. If the child is unable to discover for himself how to get the pellet from the

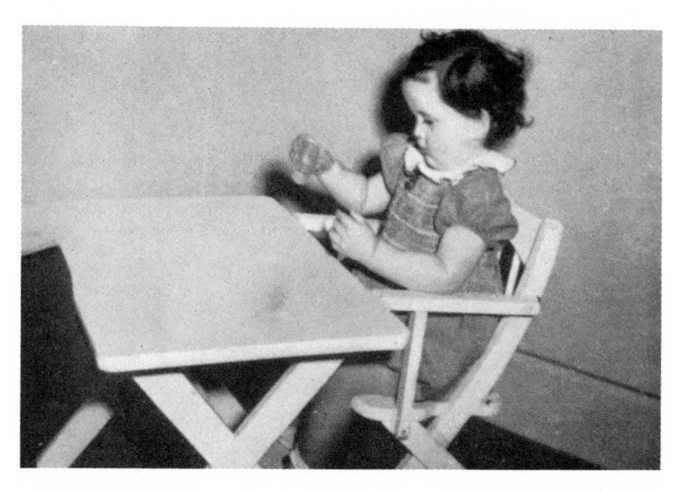

bottle, it is emptied out and put back in several times while he is watching, then the bottle is placed before him with the words, "Now —— get it."

Scoring: Credit is given if the child is able to solve the problem without demonstration or other help. (Credit is given at fourteen months if he gets the pellet out in a purposeful manner after demonstration.)

16 Months

5. Closes Round Box

Material: A round box. (See page 192.)

Procedure: The box is opened and shut several times while the child is watching. Then the box and cover are placed side by side before the child, the cover to his right (unless he is known to have a preference for his left hand). The examiner then says, "Now ——— shut the box." If he does not respond, a second demonstration may be given. If the child is still uninterested, a small object, such as a bead or a stone, is put into the box and the box shut. The box is then opened again and the cover placed

beside it in front of the child. The object is handed to the child with the words, "Now put it in the box." If he does not do so almost at once then he is helped by the examiner putting the object in the box and pointing to the cover and saying, "Shut the box."

Scoring: Credit is given if the child succeeds in closing the box. (He is given credit at fourteen months for opening the box and at twenty-two months for shutting an oblong box.)

16 Months

Alternate a. Completes Peg Board A, When Urged

Material: Wallin's Peg Board A. The board is fourteen inches long, three inches wide and three-fourths of an inch thick, with a row of six holes six-sixteenths of an inch in diameter down the center. The pegs are two and one-half inches long and are just small enough to fit in the holes without binding.

Procedure: The procedure used is similar to that used in the Merrill Palmer Scale of Mental Tests. The board is placed before the child so that the holes can be readily reached. While the child is watching, the pegs are removed and placed in a row between him and the board. He is then asked to, "See if you can put them all back in their holes." If there is no response, the examiner points first to the pegs then the board, saying "——— put them back in the holes." If there is still no response, the child is urged further by handing him a peg and saying, "Put it in here," pointing to a hole. "Put one in this hole, too." "Here's another, put it in here," etc. At the sixteen-month level he may be given any amount of encouragement, but no help in actually placing the pegs. The removing of the pegs is discouraged by such words as "Put this one in," pointing to or handing him another peg, or, "Put them all in," but he is not actually told not to take them out. The largest number in place at one time should be recorded.

Scoring: Credit is given if all six pegs are inserted and left standing at one time. (Credit is given at fourteen months if one peg is pulled out and reinserted twice and at eighteen months if all six pegs are placed without urging.)

16 Months

Alternate b. SCRIBBLES IN IMITATION

Material: Pencil and paper. (See page 178.)

Procedure: A pencil and a piece of paper are placed before the child with the words, "——— write." If after five or ten seconds he has not made any attempt to scribble, the pencil and paper are taken up and again placed before him with the same request. If there is still no response the pencil is taken from the child and a demonstration given by scribbling up and down six or eight times, making lines about three inches long. The pencil is again placed before

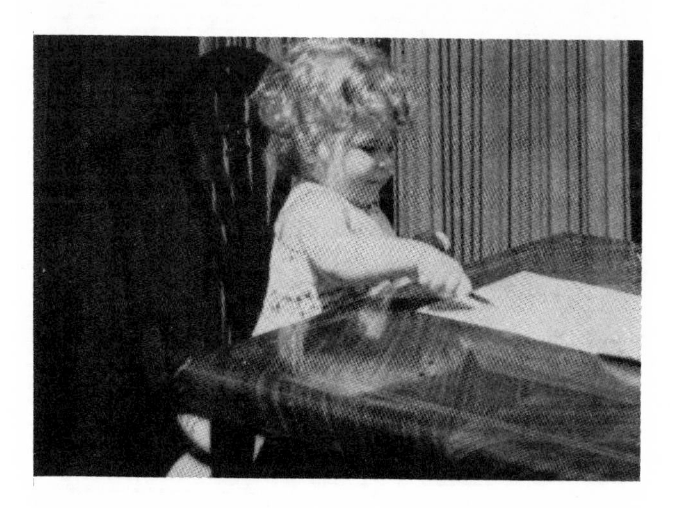

the child with the words, "———— write." The demonstration may be repeated if need be.

Scoring: Credit is given if the child takes the pencil and makes visible scribbling back and forth or circular marks either before or after the demonstration. (If he merely makes a few marks on the paper he is credited at twelve months, and if he scribbles without demonstration credit is given at eighteen months.)

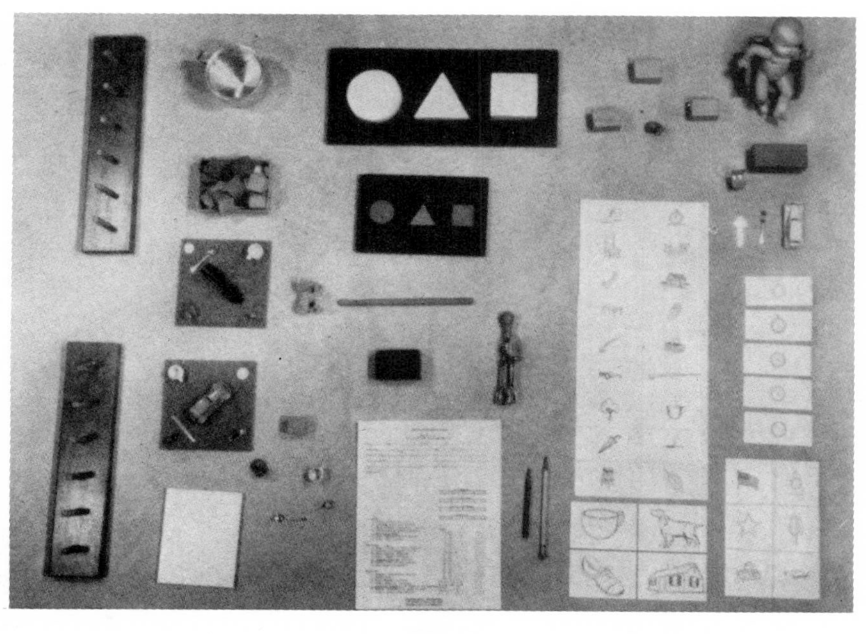

Test materials for ages eighteen to thirty months inclusive.

18 Months

1. Places Ten Cubes in Cup

Material: An aluminum cup with straight edges. Both the depth and the diameter of the rim are approximately three and one-half inches, and ten one-inch cubes painted bright red.

Procedure: The cup and a cube are placed on the table before the child with the words: "Put the block in the cup." While giving the instructions the examiner points first to the cube and then to the cup. This may be repeated two or three times. If there is still no satisfactory response, the examiner picks up the cube and places it in the cup while the child is watching.

Then, replacing the cube beside the cup to the right of the child or, when it is known, on the side of the child's favored hand, the examiner says, "——— do" (using the child's name). The demonstration may be repeated. If the child is successful, nine more cubes are pushed toward him with the instructions, "Put them all in." No further help is given.

Scoring: Credit is given if the child at any time has all ten cubes in the cup. (He is given credit at twelve months if he releases one cube into the cup.)

18 Months

2. Points to Parts of Doll

Material: Jointed rubber doll about seven inches long with legs movable at the hips.

Procedure: The jointed doll is shown the child and he is asked: "Show me the dolly's hair." This is done for (b) mouth, (c) ears, (d) hands, (e) eyes, (f) feet and (g) nose.

Scoring: Credit is given if the child is able to point out one part. (He is given credit at twenty months if he can point out three parts.)

18 Months

3. Places Circle in Rotated Formboard

Material: Large three-hole formboard. (See page 194.)

Procedure: The formboard is placed before the child with the circle on his left and the base of the triangle toward him.

1. The circle is placed in its recess and the child allowed to take it out. Then the examiner says, "Now put it back."

2. If the child is successful in placing the block in its recess with a purposeful action, the examiner takes it from its recess and returns it to the child saying, "Look." While the child is watching, the board is slowly turned in a semicircle so that the circle is on the right, and the child is asked to, "Now put it back in its hole." If he is unsuccessful, another trial should be given.

3. Next the board is again replaced in its original position with the base of the triangle toward the child and the circle on his left. The square is then placed in its recess. The child is allowed to remove it and then is asked to "Put it back in its hole." The hole is not pointed out to him, nor is he given any other help. Two or three trials may be given.

Scoring: Credit is given if the child adjusts his action to the changed position of the board and replaces the round block. Credit is not given if he finally gets the block placed after a period of trial and error. It must be placed in a purposeful manner in at least one of the three trials. (Credit is given at sixteen months for placing the round block in its recess when the board has not been turned and at twenty months for placing the square.)

18 Months

4. Scribbles Spontaneously

Material: Pencil and paper. (See page 178.)

Procedure: A pencil and a piece of paper are placed before the child with the words, "——— (child's name) write." If he does not attempt to scribble after five or ten seconds, the pencil and paper are removed and again placed before him with the same request. If there is still no response the pencil is taken from him and a demonstration given by scribbling six or eight lines up and down, making the lines about three inches long. The pencil is then again placed before the child with the words, "——— write."

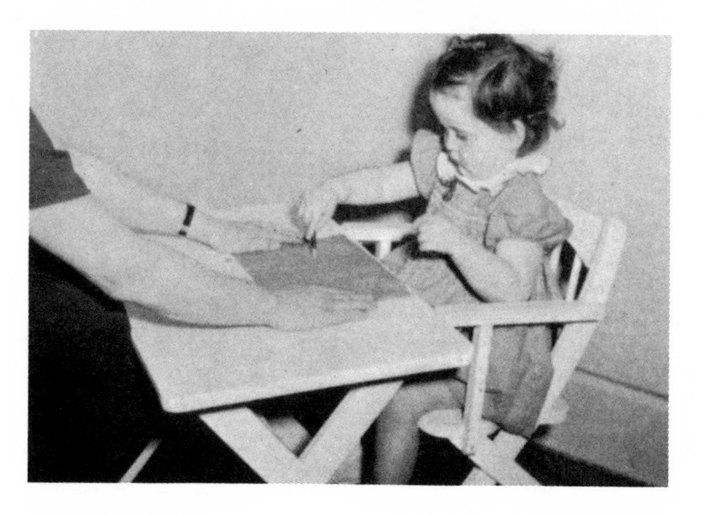

The demonstration may be repeated if need be. It should always be made with the same pencil which the child is to use and handed to him immediately after the demonstration. A child of this age may completely forget that he is holding a pencil or it may never occur to him that it would be possible to do as the examiner does without the same pencil.

Scoring: Credit is given if the child scribbles spontaneously without demonstration. (He is given credit at sixteen months if he scribbles after the demonstration.)

18 Months

5. Identifies Pictures from Name—One

Material: Two cards eight by six inches, one with pictures of a dog, a cup, a shoe, and a house; and the other with pictures of a flag, a clock, a star, a leaf, a basket and a book.

Procedure: The card with the dog, etc., is presented to the child, saying, "Where is the doggie? Show me the doggie (bow-wow)." If there is no immediate response the child is asked to "Put your finger on the doggie." The shoe, cup and house are asked for in the same manner. The other card is then presented and the objects asked for in the following order: clock, basket, book, flag, leaf and star. At times the child will point to one or two pictures and then he will stop. It is often difficult to determine whether he is refusing or whether to comply is beyond his ability. If the examiner goes back to one of the pictures the child has already named it helps both in restoring the child's confidence and in determining whether or not his failure to point out the objects is the result of inability. The object called for is sometimes recognized by a child, but either through shyness or lack of understanding of the meaning of "show me" or "put your finger on" he does not respond appropriately. Often a child who will not respond to "put your finger on," etc., will "kiss the doggie" or "put the block on the doggie." Such a response is always accepted. When there is doubt as to whether or not the child listened to the instructions, they are not repeated at once, but the next picture is asked for with the words, "Now show me the ———," and the picture to which the doubtful response was given is returned to later. If the child can talk and has failed to point to the pictures, it is permissible to point to the pictures saying, "What's that?"

Scoring: Credit is given if the child points to or names one or more pictures. (Credit is given at 22 months for pointing out two pictures.)

18 Months

Alternate a. Uses Words To Make Wants Known

Procedure: It is determined by questioning the mother (or attendant) whether the child uses words in making his wants known.

Scoring: Credit is given if the child asks for at least two things by appropriate words. Such words as "me," "more," "givme," etc., are not credited.

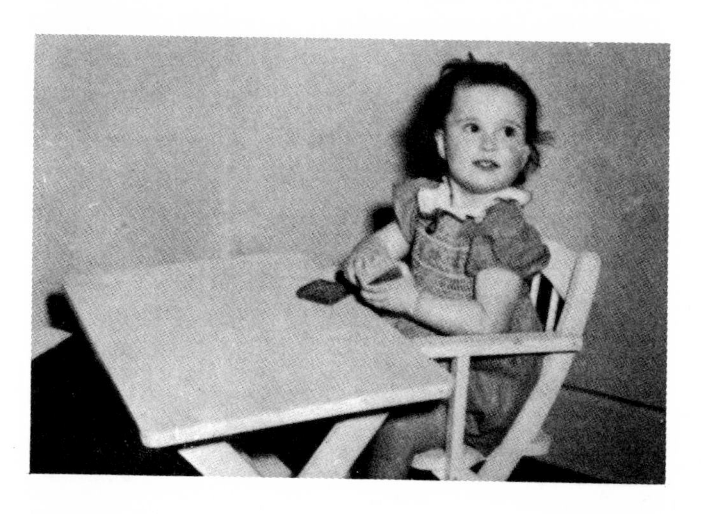

18 Months

Alternate b. Completes Peg Board A without Urging

Material: Wallin Peg Board A. (See page 144.)

Procedure: The procedure used is similar to that used in the Merrill Palmer Scale of Mental Tests. The board is placed before the child so that he can reach the holes. The pegs are removed and placed in a row before the child as he watches. Then the child is asked to, "See if you can put them back in their holes." If he does not respond, point first to the pegs, then to the board saying, "——— put them back." At this level no other help is given except verbal encouragement such as "that's fine," "put another one in," "put them all in," etc.

Scoring: Credit is given if all six pegs are placed in the holes. (Credit is given at sixteen months if the child gets all the pegs in with the additional help of being handed some of the pegs and having the holes pointed out.)

20 Months

1. Builds Tower of Three Cubes

Material: Ten one-inch cubes painted red.

Procedure: Ten cubes are placed in a pile before the child. The examiner builds a tower of two or three cubes, at the same time asking and motioning the child to do the same. If he does not do so, he may be handed the blocks one at a time with the words: "Put it on here" "—— make one here." Pointing to another, "Here is another, put it on too. Make a big house," etc. Several demonstration towers may be built by the examiner, but care must be taken not to arouse the child's interest in knocking down

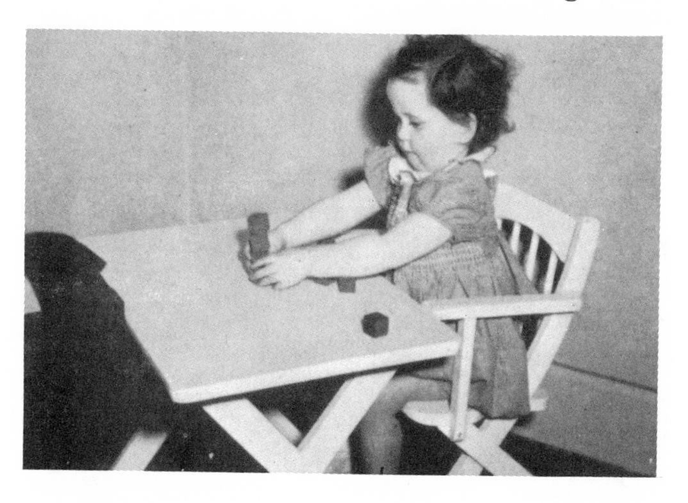

rather than building up the towers. A somewhat similar item is placed at two years in the new Stanford-Binet scale. The procedure used here has been modified in order to bring the item down to a lower age level.

Scoring: Credit is given if the tower stands at three blocks or if the child adds two blocks to the demonstration tower. The tower must stand unsupported after the third block has been placed and the hands removed. (Credit is given at sixteen months for a tower of two blocks.)

20 Months

2. Places Square in Formboard

Material: Large three-hole formboard. (See page 194.)

Procedure: The formboard is placed before the child with the circle on the left and the base of the triangle toward him. The circle is placed in its recess and the child is allowed to take it out. Then he is asked with an appropriate gesture to, "Now put it back." If the child is successful in placing the block with a purposeful act, it is taken from its recess and returned to the child saying, "Look." While the child is watching, the board is slowly turned so that the

circle is on the right, and the child is asked to "Now put it back in its hole." If he is unsuccessful, give another trial. For the square, the board is replaced in its original position with the base of the triangle toward the child and the circle on his left. The square is placed in its recess. The child is allowed to remove it. Then he is asked to "Put it back in its hole." The hole is not pointed out to him, nor is he given any other help.

Scoring: Credit is given if the child replaces the square block in its recess with purposeful movements. (He is given credit for replacing the circle in the reversed board at eighteen months.)

20 Months

3. Attains Toy with Stick

Material: A round stick eight inches long and about three-eighths of an inch in diameter and a toy dog, about two inches long, made of a pipe cleaner.

Procedure: The pipe-cleaner dog is placed on the table in front of the child just out of his reach, with the stick touching the dog and pointing toward the child. If an attempt is made to reach the dog without use of the stick, the examiner says, as he moves to the child's side of the table, "No, see how I make the doggie come?" The examiner pulls the dog toward the

child by means of the stick saying, "Come doggie." The dog and stick are then replaced with the words, "——— make the doggie come."

Scoring: Credit is given if the child makes a purposeful attempt to attain the dog by means of the stick, even if he should fail to secure the dog on account of lack of muscular coordination.

20 Months

4. Attempts to Follow Directions

Material: Jointed doll (see page 210), an arm chair to fit the doll, a small doll's cup and a small handkerchief.

Procedure: The chair is placed before the child and the doll seated beside it.

a. The examiner says to the child, "Put the doll in the chair. Dolly wants to sit in the chair." If an earnest attempt to carry out the command is made by the child, but he is unable to get the doll seated on account of poor muscular coordination, he is assisted and credited with this part of the item. If only a feeble attempt is

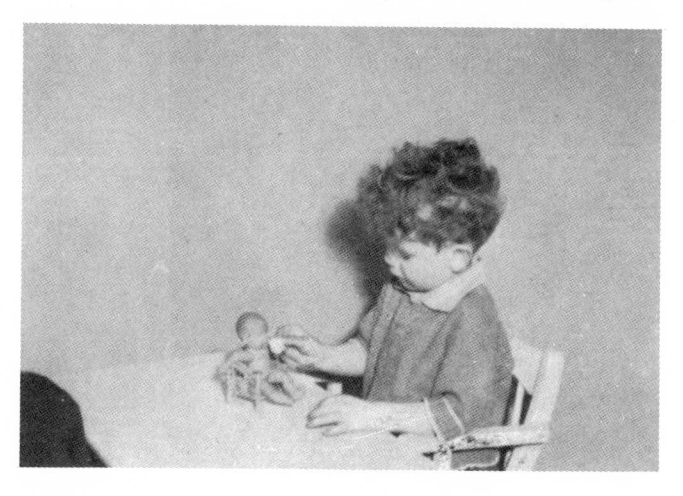

made, or none at all, the doll is placed in the chair by the examiner, but no credit is given.

b. Next the child is handed the cup with the words, "Dolly wants a drink. Give dolly a drink." He is credited if he tips the cup in the general vicinity of the face or upper part of the body. Anywhere between the top of the forehead and the navel is satisfactory. Occasionally the child refuses on the ground that there is no water in the cup. A few tiny pieces of paper put in the cup are usually enough to satisfy him.

c. The child is handed a handkerchief with the words, "Here is a handkerchief. Wipe the dolly's nose." The child is credited if he wipes in the general vicinity of the nose.

Scoring: Credit is given if two of the three parts are passed.

20 Months

5. Points to Parts of Doll

Material: Jointed doll. (See page 210.)

Procedure: The jointed doll is presented to the child with the words, "Show me the dolly's hair." If there is no response, "Where is the dolly's hair, put your finger on her hair," is added. The same procedure is used for (b) mouth, (c) ears, (d) hands, (e) eyes, (f) feet, and (g) nose.

Scoring: Credit is given if the child is able to point out at least three parts. (He is given credit for one part at eighteen months and for five at twenty-two months.)

20 Months

Alternate a. Selects Box Containing Toy

Material: Three small boxes about one and three-fourths by one and one-half by one inches and a toy cat small enough to be readily covered by the boxes.

Procedure: The boxes are placed in a row about three inches apart. The examiner says, "Look I'm going to hide the kitty and then see if you can find it again." Care must be taken to see that the child is watching as the cat is hidden first (a) under the middle box, then (b) under the box to the child's left and finally (c) under the box to the child's right. The examiner counts aloud from one to ten at the rate of one per second while the child's hands are gently held by the mother or examiner. Then his hands are released and he is asked to, "Now find the kitty." The child's first choice in each trial is the one that is scored. This item is based on the delayed response in Form M of the Stanford-Binet, but has been modified to bring it down to the 20-month level.

Scoring: Credit is given if the child makes the correct response in two out of the three trials. If in any trial the examiner has been unable to prevent two boxes from being turned simultaneously, that trial is scored minus.

20 Months

Alternate b. Completes Peg Board B without Urging

Material: Wallin Peg Board B. This peg board is similar to A except that the holes are five-sixteenth of an inch square instead of round. (See page 144.)

Procedure: The procedure used is similar to that used in the Merrill Palmer Scale of mental tests. The board is placed before the child so that the holes are within easy reach. While the child is watching the pegs are removed and placed in a row between the board and the edge of the table. The child is then asked to, "See if you can put them back in their holes." If there is no response the examiner points to the pegs, then to the board, saying, "——— put them back." At this level no other help is given except verbal encouragement such as "That's fine, put another one in. Put them all in," etc.

Scoring: Credit is given if all six pegs are placed in the holes without help.

22 Months

1. Closes Oblong Box

Material: An oblong box approximately two and one half by one and three fourths by one and one half inches with square corners. The sides of the cover should not extend to the bottom of the box. The cover should be sufficiently loose to enable it to slide off and on with little friction and sufficiently sturdy to avoid breaking when the child makes clumsy efforts to force the cover into place.

Procedure: The box is opened and shut several times while the child is watching. Then the box and cover are placed side by side before

him, the cover with the top side up and on the side of the child's preferred hand, then he is instructed to, "Now ——— shut the box" (using the child's name). Several trials may be given. If there is doubt as to which is the child's preferred hand, the side on which the cover is placed should be alternated. If there is any need to stimulate his interest further, the child may be given an object to place in the box, as in the round box. However, at this age level almost all children are interested in shutting and opening boxes. Additional incentives are seldom needed.

Scoring: Credit is given is the child shuts the box at least twice.

22 Months

2. Joins Two Words

Procedure: It is determined whether or not the child can put two words together with two meanings such as "shut door," "daddy gone." Two words denoting only one concept, such as "bye-bye," "all gone," etc., are not credited. "Good girl" when first spoken usually refers to a specific act in which case it is not credited as combining two words, but should it be used to mean approved behavior in several situations as distinguished from unapproved behavior it should be given credit.

Scoring: Credit is given if the child in his talk can put two concepts into one sentence or phrase.

22 Months

3. Stanford-Binet Formboard*

Material: Small three-hole formboard used by Terman and Merrill.

Procedure: The procedure is as in the Stanford-Binet. The board is presented with the blocks in place so that the base of the triangle will be toward the child. The examiner asks the child to "Watch what I do," as he removes the blocks and places each before its appropriate recess on the side toward the child. Then he says, "Now put them back into their holes." Two trials are allowed. The blocks are returned to the board for a second trial and the procedure repeated. It is counted as a trial when the child has arranged the pieces to his satisfaction as indicated by pushing back the board or looking up at the examiner.

Scoring: Credit is given if all three blocks are correctly placed in one of the two trials.

---

* This is the first of the items taken directly from Form L of the Stanford-Binet without modification. Unless otherwise noted all items taken from Form L of the Stanford-Binet are given and scored exactly as prescribed by Doctors Terman and Merrill, thus making it possible to use them without regiving in scoring either the present test or the Stanford-Binet.

22 Months

4. Identifies Pictures from Name—Two

Material: Two cards with pictures. (See page 215.)

Procedure: The card with the dog, etc., is presented to the child, saying, "Where is the doggie? Show me the doggie (bow-wow)." If there is no immediate response the child is asked to "Put your finger on the doggie." The shoe, cup, and house are asked for in order. The other card is then presented, beginning with the clock, basket, book, flag, leaf and star. At times one or two pictures are pointed out by the child and then he will stop. It is often difficult to

determine whether the response is a refusal or inability to perform the task. If the examiner goes back to one of the pictures he has already named, it helps both in restoring the child's confidence and in determining whether or not his failure to point out the objects is the result of inability. The object called for is sometimes recognized by a child, but either through shyness or lack of understanding of the meaning of "show me" or "put your finger on" he does not respond appropriately. Often a child who will not respond to "put your finger on," etc., will "kiss the doggie" or "put the block on the doggie." Such a response is always accepted. The request is not repeated at once when there is doubt as to whether or not the child listened to the directions, but he is asked for the next picture with, "Now show me the ———," and the picture to which the doubtful response was given is returned to later. If the child can talk and has failed to point to the pictures, it is permissible to point to the picture and say, "What's that?"

Scoring: Credit is given if the child points to or names correctly at least two pictures. (He is given credit for one at eighteen months, six at twenty-seven months and seven at thirty months.)

22 Months

5. Attempts to Follow Directions

Material: Jointed doll, cup, chair and handkerchief. (See pages 210 and 225.)

Procedure: The chair is placed before the child and the doll seated beside it.

a. The child is told to "Put the doll in the chair. Dolly wants to sit in the chair." If the child makes a persistent attempt to carry out the command, but is unable to get the doll seated on account of poor muscular coordination, he is assisted and credited with this part of the item. If only a feeble attempt it made, or none at all, the doll is placed in the chair by the examiner, but no credit given.

b. Next the child is handed the cup with the words, "Dolly wants a drink. Give dolly a drink." He is credited if he tips the cup in the general vicinity of the face or upper part of the body. Anywhere between the top of the forehead and the navel is satisfactory. Occasionally the child refuses on the ground that there is no water in the cup. A few tiny pieces of paper put in the cup are usually enough to satisfy him.

c. The child is handed a handkerchief saying, "Here is a handkerchief, wipe the dolly's nose." The child is credited if he wipes in the general vicinity of the nose.

Scoring: Credit is given if all three parts are passed. (Credit is given for two parts at 20 months.)

22 Months

Alternate a. Points to Parts of Doll

Material: Jointed doll. (See page 210.)

Procedure: The jointed doll is shown to the child with the words, "Show me the dolly's hair." If there is no immediate response he is asked, "Where is the dolly's hair? Put your finger on her hair." He is then asked to point out (b) mouth, (c) ears, (d) hands, (e) eyes, (f) feet, and (g) nose.

Scoring: Credit is given if the child is able to point out five parts. (Credit is given for one part at eighteen months and three at twenty months.)

22 Months

Alternate b. STANFORD-BINET IDENTIFYING OBJECT BY NAME

Material: Card with six small objects attached: cat, button, thimble, cup, spoon, engine.

Procedure: This test is taken from the Stanford-Binet, Form L, and the same procedure is followed. The card with the six small objects attached is shown to the child with the words, "See all these things? Show me the kitty. Put your finger on the kitty. Where is the kitty?" The examiner then asks for the objects in the following order: (b) button, (c) thimble, (d) cup, (e) engine (train, choo-choo), (f) spoon. It is not permissible to ask for the objects by any special names other than those specified.

Scoring: Credit is given if the child designates correctly two objects by pointing. (He is given credit at twenty-four months if he identifies four objects.)

24 Months

1. Stanford-Binet Identifying Object by Name

Material: Card with six small objects attached: cat, button, thimble, cup, spoon and engine.

Procedure: This test is taken from the Stanford-Binet, Form L, and the same procedure is followed. The card with the six small objects attached is shown to the child with the words "See all these things? Show me the kitty. Put your finger on the kitty. Where is the kitty?" The examiner asks for the other objects in the following order: (a) kitty, (b) button, (c) thimble, (d) cup, (e) engine (train, choo-choo), (f) spoon. It is not permissible to ask for the objects by any special names other than those specified.

Scoring: Credit is given if the child designates correctly four objects by pointing. (He is given credit if he identifies two objects at twenty-two months.)

24 Months

2. Attempts to Fold Paper

Material: Two sheets of paper four and one-half by five and one-half inches.

Procedure: The procedure is taken from the Merrill Palmer Scale. The only difference is that in this test two demonstrations may be given. The examiner shows a sheet of paper to the child saying, "Watch what I do. I am going to make a book. See. I fold it over this way and then press it down like this and it makes a little book." The paper is shown double, and then while the fold is being opened and closed, the examiner says, "Isn't this a nice little book?

See if you can make a little book out of this paper," handing the child a similar bit of paper. A second demonstration may be given if the child has made no attempt to fold the paper.

Scoring: Credit is given if the child turns up the paper in an attempt to fold it, even if he does not succeed in making a definite crease. (If he makes a definite crease he is given credit at thirty months.)

24 Months

3. Recognizes Incomplete Watch

Material: Five pictures of a watch one inch in diameter in various stages of completion, each one on a separate small card.

Procedure: The first picture is shown to the child saying, "What is that?" If there is no answer, the procedure is repeated, but this should not be urged to the extent of disturbing the child. He is shown the next picture and asked again, "What is that?" The procedure is continued with the other pictures until the last one has been shown or until the child has named the watch. "Tick-tick" or "clock" is considered correct.

Scoring: Credit is given if the child names the watch on the third picture or before.

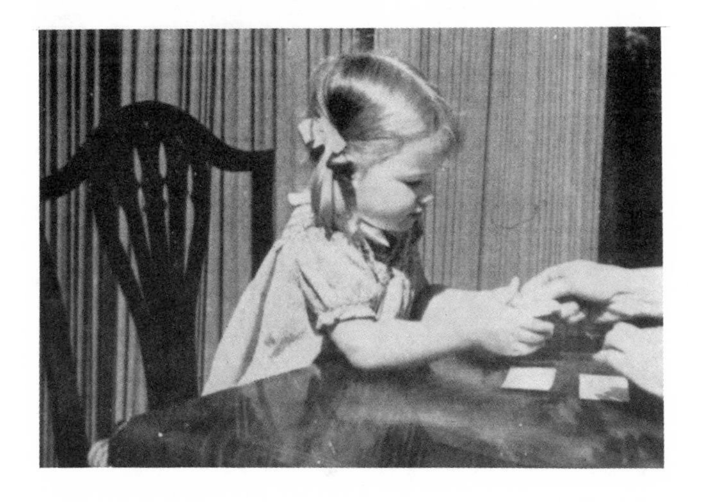

24 Months

4. Stanford-Binet Simple Commands

Material: Block, spoon, cat, cup and thimble.

Procedure: This item is taken from Form L of the Stanford-Binet, the procedure of which is as follows. The objects are placed in a row on the table in the following order, block, spoon, cat, cup, thimble, and the child is asked to

a. "Give me the kitty."
b. "Put the spoon in the cup."
c. "Put the thimble on the block."

The objects are replaced in the same order after each trial. It is sometimes necessary for each

command to be repeated several times if the child has made no move toward carrying out the request.

Scoring: Credit is given if the child responds correctly to two of the three commands. (Credit is given at forty-two months in Form L of the Stanford-Binet if all three commands are carried out correctly.)

24 Months

5. Stanford-Binet Naming Objects

Material: Chair, automobile, box, key and fork.

Procedure: This test is taken from Form L of the Stanford-Binet, the procedure of which is to present the objects one at a time with the question, "What is this? What do you call it?" The objects should be presented in the following order: (a) chair, (b) automobile, (c) box, (d) key, and (e) fork.

Scoring: Credit is given if the child names three objects correctly. (Credit is given at 27 months for naming four objects correctly.)

24 Months

Alternate a. Stanford-Binet Picture Vocabulary

Material: Eighteen two by four inch cards with pictures of common objects.

Procedure: This test is taken from the Stanford-Binet, the procedure of which is to show the cards one at a time and ask, "What's this?" "What do you call it?"

Scoring: Credit is given if the child names three pictures correctly. (Credit is given for one at twenty-two months, for seven at twenty-seven months and for ten at thirty months.)

24 Months

Alternate b. PLACES CUBES IN BOX

Material: Twelve one-inch cubes, painted bright red, and a box with inside measurements of three and one-eighth by four and one-eighth inches. The box should be made of wood or some other strong material. A child in forcing the cubes into place will soon tear apart an ordinary cardboard box. A heavy cardboard box reinforced on the outside with adhesive tape gives fairly satisfactory results.

Procedure: After one of the cube tests has been completed, the box is placed before the child with the words, "Now, let's put them back in the box." If the child does not begin at once, one or two cubes are placed in the box by the examiner. If the child piles the blocks on top of one another, the examiner points to one that is in place and says, "No, put them down in the box like this so that they are all the way in." Or, if not more than five blocks have been placed, the examiner may take one that has been piled on top of another and place it in the box saying, "Like this, see?" If the child still fails to understand the test is scored as a failure.

Scoring: Credit is given if all twelve blocks are placed in the box.

27 Months

1. Makes Train of Cubes

Material: Ten one-inch cubes. (See page 108.)

Procedure: The examiner empties ten cubes on the table, then places four in a row saying, "Look how I make a train, like this, and this, and this, and this, and here is the engine" placing a fifth cube on top of the first. "See how it goes." The examiner pushes it about the table, saying, "Choo-choo-choo." Five other cubes are pushed toward the child with the request, "You make one. You make a train (choo-choo) like mine."

Scoring: Credit is given if the child puts at least three blocks in a row and pushes them about.

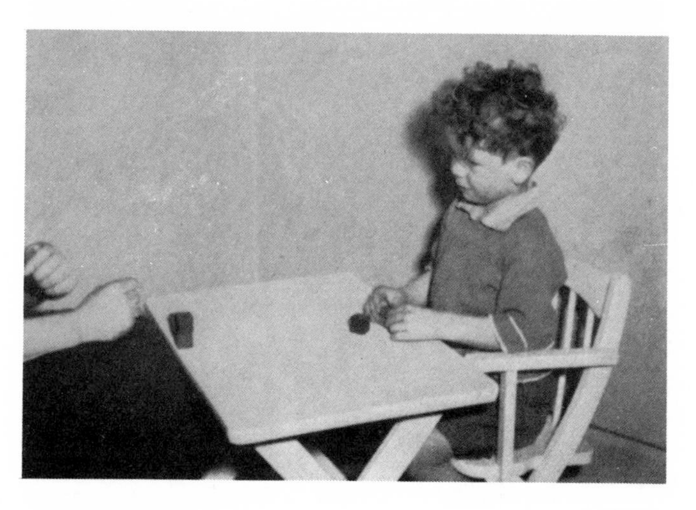

27 Months

2. Stanford-Binet Motor Coordination

Material: Toy egg-beater, five and one-half inches long.

Procedure: This test is taken from Form M of the Stanford-Binet, the procedure of which is to demonstrate several revolutions saying, "See this. You make it go the way I do." The egg-beater is presented in position for the child's preferred hand. Three trials are given with a demonstration before each trial.

Scoring: Credit is given if the child makes one complete turn of the handle in any of the trials.

27 Months

3. Imitates Drawing Line

Material: Pencil and paper. (See page 178.)

Procedure: The examination form or a piece of paper is placed before the child and a three-inch vertical stroke directed toward the child is made on it with a pencil and the pencil presented with the words, "——— make one like that." The pencil is taken again and a horizontal three-inch line made from the child's left to his right. The pencil is returned with the words, "Now, make one just like this." The pencil is taken again and two or three concentric circles are made by the examiner and the

pencil returned to the child with the request, "Now make one like this." If the child fails on any part of the item, all three parts must be repeated, beginning with the vertical stroke.

Scoring: Credit is given if the child succeeds in making a stroke as distinct from a scribble. (If he differentiates between the horizontal and vertical line and also the line and the circle he is given credit at thirty months.)

27 Months

4. Stanford-Binet Picture Vocabulary

Material: Eighteen cards two by four inches with pictures of common objects, used in Form L of the Stanford-Binet.

Procedure: The cards are shown one at a time with the question, "What's this? What do you call it?"

Scoring: Credit is given if the child names seven pictures correctly. (Credit is given for one picture at twenty-two months, three at twenty-four months.)

27 Months

5. Identifies Pictures from Name

Material: Two cards with pictures. (See page 215.)

Procedure: The card with the dog, etc., is presented to the child, saying, "Where is the doggie? Show me the doggie (bow-wow)." If there is no immediate response, the child is asked to "Put your finger on the doggie." The shoe, cup and house are asked for in order. The other card is then presented and the clock, basket, book, flag, leaf and star are asked for in order. At times the child will name one or two pictures and then stop. It is often difficult to

determine whether the response is a refusal or inability to perform the task. If the examiner goes back to one of the pictures he has already named, it helps both in restoring the child's confidence and in determining whether or not his failure to point out the objects is the result of inability. The object called for is sometimes recognized by the child, but either through shyness or lack of understanding of the meaning of "show me" or "put your finger on" he does not respond appropriately. Often a child who will not respond to "put your finger on," etc., will "kiss the doggie" or "put the block on the doggie." Such a response should always be accepted. When there is doubt as to whether or not he listened to the directions he is asked for the next picture with, "Now show me the ————," and the picture to which the doubtful response was given is returned to later. If the child can talk and has failed to point to the pictures, it is permissible to point to the pictures saying, "What's that?"

Scoring: Credit is given if the child points correctly to at least six pictures. (Credit is given for two at twenty-two months and for seven at thirty months.)

27 Months

Alternate a. Stanford-Binet Naming Objects

Material: Chair, automobile, box, key and fork.

Procedure: This test is taken from Form L of the Stanford-Binet, the procedure of which is to present the objects one at a time. The child is asked, "What is this? What do you call it?" The items (a) chair, (b) automobile, (c) box, (d) key and (e) fork, are presented in order.

Scoring: Credit is given if the child names four objects correctly. (Credit is given for three objects at twenty-four months.)

27 Months

Alternate b. Repeats Two Digits

Procedure: After the child's attention has been obtained, the examiner says, "Listen; say 2," "now say 4 – 7," now say (b) 6 – 3, (c) 5 – 8. The digits must be pronounced distinctly and with perfectly uniform emphasis at the rate of one per second.

Scoring: Credit is given if any one of the three sets of numbers is repeated in correct order without error.

30 Months

1. Differentiates Bridge from Tower

Material: Twelve one-inch red cubes. (See page 108.)

Procedure: After the tower test, the examiner says, "Now we are going to make one like this," at the same time building a three-cube bridge with a space between the two base blocks. Then, pointing to the blocks before the child, he says, "——— make one." Several demonstration bridges may be built. If the tower test was given earlier in the examination it must be repeated just before the bridge test is given.

Scoring: Credit is given if the child shows in

his attempt to build the bridge that he differentiates between it and the tower built just previously. The actual successful building of the bridge does not come until later and is placed at thirty-six months by Terman and Merrill in the Stanford-Binet.

30 Months

2. IMITATES DRAWING LINES AND CIRCLES

Material: Pencil and paper. (See page 178.)

Procedure: The examination form or a piece of paper is placed before the child and a three-inch vertical stroke directed toward the child is made on it with a pencil and the pencil handed to the child with the words, "——— make one like that." The pencil is taken again by the examiner and a horizontal three-inch line made from the child's left to right. The pencil is returned to the child, saying, "Now, make one just like this." The pencil is taken again and two or three concentric circles are made by the exam-

iner and the pencil returned to the child with the request, "Now make one like this." If the child fails on any part of the test, the item should be repeated on another sheet of paper. If the test is repeated at all, the whole test must be repeated, beginning with the vertical stroke.

Scoring: Credit is given if the child differentiates both between the horizontal and vertical strokes and between the strokes and the circle. In order to receive credit for differentiation between the vertical and horizontal strokes, the strokes must be within 20° of vertical and horizontal, respectively, and the lesser angle between the two lines must be at least 60°. The child is not expected at this age to be able to copy a circle; any circular or up-and-down motion of the pencil which is definitely differentiated from the strokes is scored plus. If the child fails in imitating a stroke, this item is scored minus. (Credit is given at twenty-seven months if he succeeds in making a stroke as distinct from a scribble.)

30 Months

3. Stanford-Binet Three-Hole Formboard Rotated

(*Item 22:3 must precede this*)

Material: Small formboard. (See page 233.)

Procedure: This item must be preceded by Item 22:3 with several other items between. The procedure followed is that used in the Stanford-Binet. With the board before the child with the base of the triangle toward him, the blocks are removed while the child watches and are placed each before its proper recess on the side toward the child. Then, while the child is watching, the board is rotated to a position with the apex of the triangle toward the child and he is asked to "Put them all back where they belong." Give two trials, repeating the same procedure for the second trial.

Scoring: Credit is given if all the blocks are correctly placed in either trial.

30 Months

4. Folds Paper

Material: Two sheets of paper four and one-half by five and one-half inches.

Procedure: The procedure is taken from the Merrill Palmer Scale. The only difference is that in this test two demonstrations may be given. The examiner shows a sheet of paper to the child saying, "Watch what I do. I am going to make a book. See. I fold it over this way and then press it down like this and it makes a little book." The paper is shown double, and then while the fold is being opened and closed, the examiner says, "Isn't this a nice little book? See if you can make a little book out of this

paper," handing the child a similar bit of paper. A second demonstration may be given if the child has made no attempt to fold the paper.

Scoring: Credit is given if the child is able to make a definite crease in the paper. The direction and number of creases is disregarded, but merely crumpling the paper is not credited. (Credit is given at twenty-four months if he attempts to fold the paper even if he is unable to make a crease.)

30 Months

5. Stanford-Binet Identifying Objects by Use

Material: Card with cup, shoe, penny, knife, automobile and iron attached.

Procedure: This item is taken from the Stanford-Binet, Form L, the procedure of which is to show the card with the six small objects attached and say, "Show me the one that ...." or "Which one ...." or "Show me what ...."

a. .... we drink out of.
b. .... goes on our feet.
c. .... we can buy candy with.
d. .... we can cut with.
e. .... we ride in.
f. .... we use to iron clothes.

Scoring: Credit is given if four objects are correctly pointed out. In the Stanford-Binet three correct responses are given credit at thirty months. The explanation of the difference probably lies in the fact that in the Stanford-Binet the thirty-month items cover the age period from twenty-four to thirty months, while in the infant tests they only cover the three-month period from twenty-seven to thirty months.

30 Months

Alternate a. IDENTIFIES PICTURES FROM NAME

Material: Two cards with pictures. (See page 215.)

Procedure: The card with the dog, etc., is presented to the child, saying, "Where is the doggie? Show me the doggie (bow-wow)." If there is no immediate response, the child is asked to "Put your finger on the doggie." The shoe, cup and house are asked for in order. The other card is then presented and the clock, basket, book, flag, leaf and star are asked for in order. At times the child will point out one or two pictures and then stop. It is often difficult to determine whether the response is a refusal or inability to perform the task. If the examiner goes back to one of the pictures he has already named, it helps both in restoring the child's confidence and in determining whether or not his failure to point out the objects is the result of inability. The object called for is sometimes recognized by the child, but either through shyness or lack of understanding of the meaning of "show me" or "put your finger on" he does not respond appropriately. Often a child who will not respond to "put your finger on," etc., will "kiss the doggie" or "put the block on the doggie." Such a response should always be accepted. When there is doubt as to whether or not he listened to the directions, he is asked for the next picture with, "Now show me the ————" and the picture to which the doubtful response was given is returned to later. If the child can talk and has failed to point to the pictures, it is permissible to point to the picture, saying, "What's that?"

Scoring: Credit is given if the child points to or names correctly at least seven pictures. (Credit is given at twenty-seven months if he points to six and at twenty-two months if he points to two.)

30 Months

Alternate b. Concept of One

Material: Twelve one-inch cubes. (See page 108.)

Procedure: A piece of paper about four and one-half by five and one-half inches is placed between the examiner and the child with the words, "I want one block. I only want one. Put it here (pointing to the paper). Give me just one block." The block on the paper must not be removed until the child has had time to add another block.

Scoring: Credit is given if the child puts one and only one cube on the paper.

INDEX